Brilliant Strengths

A Strengths-Based Program
Designed to Raise Self-Esteem and
Lower Anxiety in Students with Dyslexia

BY NICKI WINTER, MED, LDT, CALT

For any additional information regarding educational needs, speaking engagements or inquiries, contact info@brilliantstrengths.com

ISBN 979-8-986-2257-0-8

Editor: Becky Noelle
Illustrator: Paul Trudeau
Photo on back cover: Brittany Davis

TO TED, TEDDY, AND SOPHIE FOR SHARING THIS JOURNEY WITH ME

AND

TO ALL STUDENTS WITH DYSLEXIA WHO SHARE THEIR JOURNEY WITH THEIR PARENTS AND TEACHERS.

YOU ARE BRILLIANT.

CONTENTS

FOREWORD BY DR. CLAUDIA BEENY

MY PARENTS MOVED ME from my local public school to a parochial school in the middle of my fourth-grade year. I was diagnosed with dyslexia months prior, and my loving parents hoped the smaller classrooms would provide me the extra attention and accommodations I needed to thrive. Because it was midyear, I started my first day without a school uniform, a seemingly small detail but paramount in the mind of a ten-year-old whose only desire was to be like everyone else. My well-intended teacher tried ensuring I would fit in by immediately calling on me to define what a pew was. She had no way of knowing I had little exposure to formalized religion and that I had no idea the answer to her question. Instead, I sat paralyzed with fear, wishing I could disappear. The combination of not knowing the answer to my teacher's question and not wearing what everyone was wearing affirmed everything I had come to believe about myself up to that point: I was different, I wasn't smart, and I stood out for all the wrong reasons.

That memory is indicative of how I experienced most of my childhood and many of my adult years. Unfortunately, being labeled dyslexic started me on a journey of feeling both self-conscious and fearful. My self-consciousness was rooted in my awareness that the basics of school were harder for me than for my classmates, and my fear came from worrying that others would find out. To protect myself, I became masterful at hiding. I hid by never answering questions in class, avoiding any activity or project where I felt put on the spot, and always observing "smarter," more confident kids before gaining the courage to try something myself.

I needed exposure to a resource just like *Brilliant Strengths* during those difficult yet formative years. Nicki Winter's practical and uplifting guide provides parents and educators the tools needed to reframe conversations for young people about what it means to be dyslexic. Rather than highlighting how students like me feel embarrassed and see school through the lens of their deficits, *Brilliant Strengths* focuses exclusively on the attributes of being different. Winter's guide showcases the biographies of accomplished men and women who, because of the way their minds work, have contributed creatively across an array of industries. Additionally, Winter's carefully curated selection of children's literature reinforces students' learning through the use of relatable characters and interesting stories. The fact that she's successfully packaged each affirming lesson into a fifteen-minute block of time is evidence of Winter's expertise.

Dyslexic students are often filled with internal questions about their competence and worth. Because of that, external evidence of one's attributes is particularly useful. Winters masterfully accounts for that too in her color-coded Bubble Map. After each lesson, students are instructed to document and code examples of one of the three attributes around which *Brilliant Strengths* is written: Resilient, Innovative, and Connecting. The resulting map is a touchstone that students and their families can refer to again and again when feeling overwhelmed and seeking a reminder of their greatest strengths.

My story ends well. Eventually I gained the confidence to go on and earn a PhD, which in turn allowed me to work with college students for the next twenty-five years. I realized during that time that most students suffer from insecurities and that the best antidote to those insecurities is a strong sense of contribution and commitment. For when we believe we are capable of making a meaningful contribution and we're committed to the cause, even the biggest obstacles become mere challenges along the way. Today I am Founder and Executive Director of House of Shine, a nonprofit headquartered in Grapevine, Texas. Our organization helps people ages five to ninety-five discover their strengths and put them to work in their communities, making the world a better and brighter place to live. This leg of my journey has lasted more than a decade, and it's been riddled with countless challenges. Luckily for me, my deep sense of contribution and commitment is only surpassed by my gratitude for what I now realize are the invaluable lessons I learned growing up dyslexic.

Winter's commitment to dyslexic students paved the way for her most recent contribution—*Brilliant Strengths*. This long-awaited tool is exactly what is needed for building students' confidence and self-worth during their most formative years.

— DR. CLAUDIA BEENY, Founder and Executive Director, House of Shine

Introduction

THE WHAT

What Is the Purpose of This Strengths-Based Program?

Dyslexia is the best thing I could ever ask for.
—William, seven-year-old student

This is a strengths-based program designed to increase self-esteem and lower anxiety in students with dyslexia by incorporating children's literature, emphasizing strengths, and focusing on inspirational people with dyslexia. The Extension part of each lesson introduces students to additional genres of children's literature, inspirational people with dyslexia, and hands-on activities. Exposure to various genres of literature will help students make a connection to a genre and encourage them to enjoy reading.

Throughout the lessons, students will develop a number of literacy and personal skills. Choose and adapt the lessons to fit your desired curricular outcomes. The following are skills that will be used during the lessons in this program:

> reading biographies, nonfiction, and various genres of literature

> making connections to people, events, and feelings

> using writing as a tool for reflection

> speaking and listening to discuss concepts in a group

> researching specific topics of interest using books and websites

> identifying personal strengths

> setting goals and celebrating achievements

> using technology as a tool in learning (e.g., speech-to-text and text-to-speech)

> practicing creativity through playing games, making artwork, and inventing

THE WHY

> I feel like I'm running a race. I'm standing still
> and everyone else is passing me by.
> —Ethan, eleven-year-old student

During my teaching credential program, one of my favorite classes was children's literature. I especially liked the study of bibliotherapy—using books to help meet the social, emotional, and mental needs of children. After receiving my credential, I taught at the elementary level. While teaching, I realized that one of my passions is helping struggling readers learn to read. At the urging of a mentor, I pursued becoming a dyslexia specialist and received my certification to be a Certified Academic Language Therapist. During the certification program, we read *Overcoming Dyslexia* by Sally Shaywitz. In her book, Shaywitz mentions the effect of dyslexia on a student's self-esteem. She encourages parents and teachers to focus on the student's strengths because students with dyslexia have "an island of weakness in a sea of strengths." I absolutely loved that focus! I had seen many struggling readers walk through my door with low self-esteem and an anxious spirit. Most had been comparing their reading weakness with the reading strengths of those around them since kindergarten. It was heartbreaking. I began to emphasize the strengths of the student not just in words but on paper. I would put the student's name in the middle of a piece of paper. Then together we would brainstorm their areas of strength and record them in bubble clouds around their name. By focusing on strengths, the students began to see themselves through a different lens. Their self-esteem started to increase and their anxiety to decrease.

While pursuing my dyslexia certification, I also pursued a master's in education and an Educational Diagnostician Certification. During my master's, I took an Introduction to Research course in which I had to use qualitative and quantitative data to answer a question. Because of my interest in the anxiety of students with dyslexia, I chose the research question "Do students with dyslexia experience higher levels of anxiety than those without dyslexia?" While writing my literature review to answer the question, I came upon the book Positive Dyslexia by Dr. Roderick Nicolson (it is now referred to as *Dyslexia 360*). Nicolson researched the strengths of people with dyslexia. In his book, he uses a diagram to show their ten most common strengths. Like Shaywitz, Nicolson emphasizes the need to focus on the strengths of people with dyslexia.

Later, I integrated my literature review into my action research paper titled "Positive Dyslexia: Effects on Lowering Anxiety with Students with Dyslexia." During the research process, I created a program incorporating children's literature (bibliotherapy), Nicolson's ten common strengths, famous people with dyslexia, and the recording of students' strengths into a color-coded Bubble Map. I started by having students and parents complete questionnaires about the students' anxiety related to reading, writing, and spelling. After the questionnaires were complete, I would start the strengths-based program. Once the program and the students' Strengths Bubble Maps were complete, I gave the questionnaires again. I collected and analyzed student and parent data from the questionnaires. The decrease in anxiety was evident not only in their responses but even more so in the smiles on their faces! It was amazing to watch!

After graduating with my master's, I continued to use this strengths-based program with my students in the public and private school setting. Through discussions and reflections, the program has since evolved to focus on the three strengths described in this book: Resilient, Innovative, and Connecting. I absolutely love focusing on and celebrating students' strengths and watching their self-esteem increase and their anxiety decrease. It is why I do what I do.

A mutual friend introduced Liz Trudeau and me. Liz shared her idea of a book with biographies of brilliant people with dyslexia (later to become *Brilliantly Dyslexic*), and I shared my strengths-based program that incorporated inspirational people with dyslexia (later to become *Brilliant Strengths*). A partnership was born! And it is our hope that you, the person holding this book, will join us in sharing these resources to increase the self-esteem of the students in your classroom or the children in your home.

THE WHO

Who Can Use This Strengths-Based Program?

What you leave behind is not what is engraved in stone monuments,
but what is woven in the lives of others.

—Pericles

This program is designed for anyone who works with struggling readers and would like to increase students' self-esteem while focusing on their strengths. This includes parents, general and special education teachers, dyslexia therapists, reading specialists, counselors, and librarians. To make directions easier to follow, I have used the word "student" throughout the lessons, but the lessons can be completed with any child in your care.

THE HOW

How Do I Use This Strengths-Based Program?

Instruction does much, encouragement everything.
—Johann Wolfgang von Goethe

This program is designed for flexibility so it easily fits into your schedule. Each lesson takes approximately fifteen minutes. Depending on your schedule, you can do one lesson each day, one each week, one every other week, or half a lesson at a time. This program includes seven parts: **Part I,** which introduces the strengths of Resilient, Innovative, and Connecting, along with the characters they represent; **Parts II, III,** and **IV,** which define each of the three strengths and include the corresponding lessons; **Part V,** which is the celebration upon completion of the program; **Part VI,** for students to explore more; and **Part VII,** for teachers and parents to discover their own strengths.

Each lesson follows the same format: materials needed for that lesson; definition of the strength being discussed; the book to share; example discussion questions to ask; the color for that recorded strength; the recommended biography to read from *Brilliantly Dyslexic*;[1] and an extension of the lesson, which provides the opportunity to connect literature, activities, or additional famous people with dyslexia.

Throughout the lessons, share your personal stories and reflections as you encourage your students to share theirs.

---

1 This guide was designed to accompany Liz Trudeau's book, *Brilliantly Dyslexia,* so each lesson includes a recommended reading from her book. The inspirational people from *Brilliantly Dyslexic* referred to in this guide demonstrate more than one strength. The part of the guide in which they are placed is organizational.

THE NOW

This program changes a child's perspective. I want to start it today.

— Pat Pomaro, Dyslexia Therapist in Grapevine, Texas

The program you are about to begin will greatly impact the lives of your students. Before starting, get copies of the following books from the library, bookstore, Audible, or Learning Ally:

Introducing the Three Strengths (Lesson 1)

Brilliantly Dyslexic by Liz Trudeau

Resilient (Lessons 2–6)

Bubble Gum Brain: Ready, Get Mindset...Grow! by Julia Cook

It's Okay to Make Mistakes by Todd Parr

Trying by Kobi Yamada

Rosie Revere, Engineer by Andrea Beaty

The Don't Worry Book by Todd Parr

For Extension Resilient resources, see page 88, 91

Innovative (Lessons 7–11)

The Most Magnificent Thing by Ashley Spires

Beautiful Oops! by Barney Saltzberg or *The Book of Mistakes* by Corinna Luyken

The Pencil by Allan Ahlberg

What If... by Samantha Berger

What Do You Do with a Problem? by Kobi Yamada

For Extension Innovative resources, see page 88-89, 91-92

Connecting (Lessons 12–16)

What Does It Mean to Be Kind? by Rana DiOrio

Thank You, Mr. Falker by Patricia Polacco

Up the Creek by Nicholas Oldland

Why Should I Listen? by Claire Llewellyn

Sofia Valdez, Future Prez by Andrea Beaty

For Extension Connecting resources, see page 90, 92-93

Celebration! (Lessons 17–18)

I Knew You Could! A Book for All the Stops in Your Life by Craig Dorfman

What the Road Said by Cleo Wade

Just Read! by Lori Degman

Explore More! (Lessons 19-20)

Inspire Your Power: An Inspirational Journal of Love and Joy for Kids with Dyslexia by Karlayna Platt

Xtraordinary People Made by Dyslexia by Kate Griggs

For Extension Explore More! resources, see page 90, 93

Parents and Teachers, Discover Your Strengths (Lesson 21)

Now, Discover Your Strengths by Marcus Buckingham and Donald Clifton

What's Your Shine? by Dr. Claudia Beeny

For Extension Parents and Teachers resources, see page 93

Part I

INTRODUCTION TO STRENGTHS

Resilient: to keep going even when something is hard, even when you make mistakes, and even when you're afraid

Innovative: to create, invent, and see things in a different way; to "think outside the box"

Connecting: to show kindness, to work together, and to communicate well with others

Introducing the Three Strengths

Materials:
> Sally Shaywitz Quote Card
> Definition Cards (Resilient, Innovative, and Connecting)
> one blank Strengths Bubble Map for each student
> example Strengths Bubble Map
> *Brilliantly Dyslexic* by Liz Trudeau

Introduction: Read the Sally Shaywitz Quote Card to the class. Tell students that they are working on learning to read, which may be their island of weakness. Then tell them that each one of them has strengths—a whole sea of them. Explain to students that during these lessons, they will practice focusing on strengths. Show students the example Strengths Bubble Map and tell them they will be discussing and recording their strengths in three main categories: Resilient, Innovative, and Connecting.

Definitions: Show students the Definition Cards (Resilient, Innovative, and Connecting) one at a time. Read out the following definitions as you discuss each card with the class (definitions are also included on the cards).

    Resilient: to keep going even when something is hard, even when you make mistakes, and even when you're afraid
    Innovative: to create, invent, and see things in a different way; to "think outside the box"
    Connecting: to show kindness, to work together, and to communicate well with others

Reflection: Have students write their names or place pictures of themselves in the center cloud of their Strengths Bubble Maps (students could also use speech-to-text in a Google Doc or Seesaw text page). Tell students they will be discussing how they demonstrate these strengths and recording their examples on their Strengths Bubble Maps throughout the lessons.

student

Brilliant People: Show students the book *Brilliantly Dyslexic.* Tell them that throughout these lessons, they will be reading biographies of incredible people with dyslexia who demonstrate these strengths.

HELPFUL HINT

Display the definition cards for reference throughout the lessons.

Students with dyslexia have "an island of weakness in a sea of strengths."

—Sally Shaywitz

ILLUSTRATION BY PAUL TRUDEAU

Resilient: to keep going even when something is hard, even when you make mistakes, and even when you're afraid

ILLUSTRATION BY PAUL TRUDEAU

Innovative: to create, invent, and see things in a different way; to "think outside the box"

Carl the Connector

ILLUSTRATION BY PAUL TRUDEAU

Connecting: to show kindness, to work together, and to communicate well with others

Blank Strengths Bubble Map

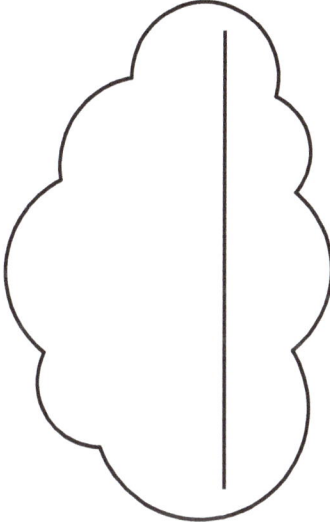

- Resilient
- Innovative
- Connecting
- Additional

Example Strengths Bubble Map

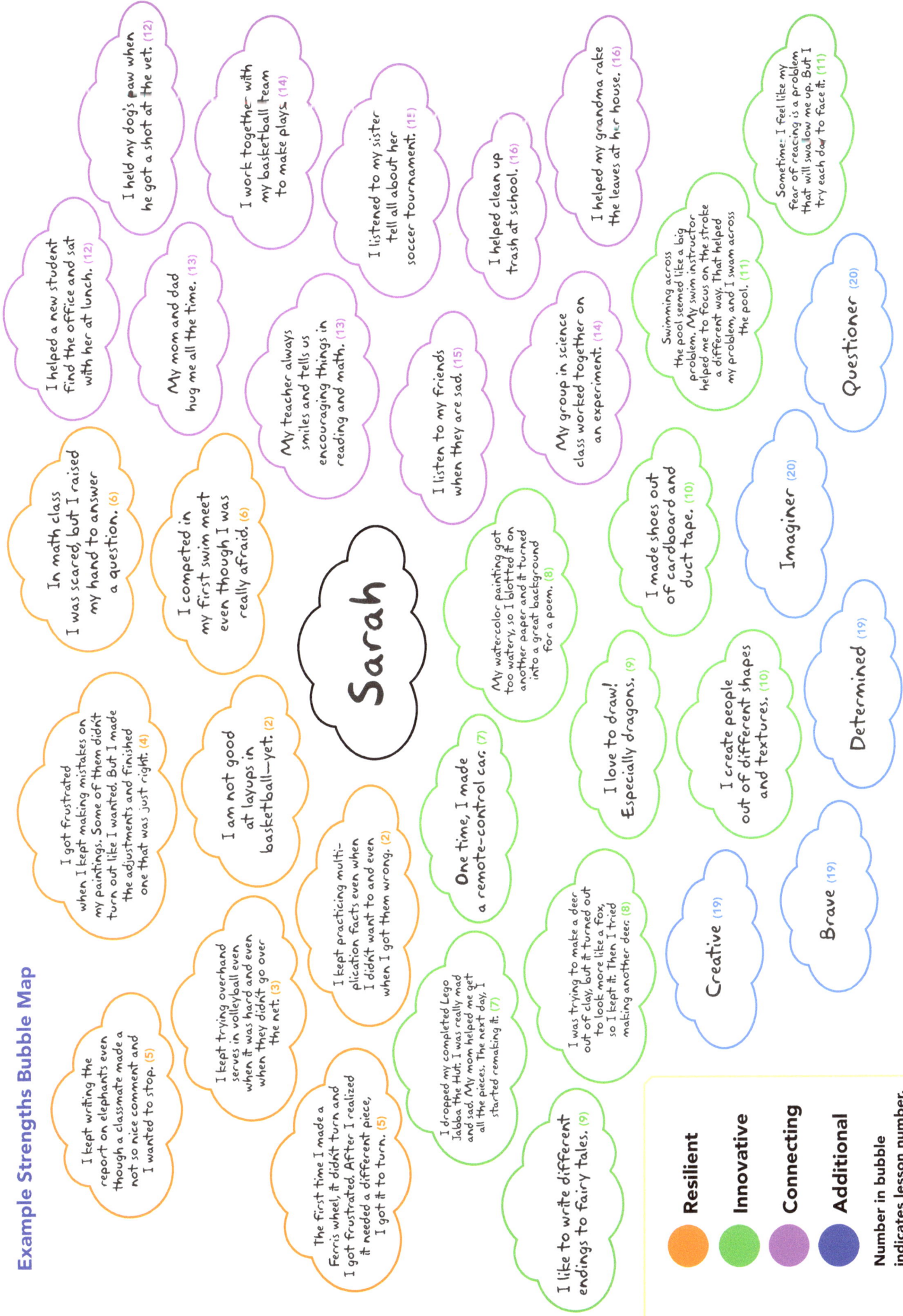

Sarah

Resilient (orange)

- In math class I was scared, but I raised my hand to answer a question. (6)
- I competed in my first swim meet even though I was really afraid. (6)
- I got frustrated when I kept making mistakes on my paintings. Some of them didn't turn out like I wanted. But I made the adjustments and finished one that was just right. (4)
- I am not good at layups in basketball—yet. (2)
- I kept writing the report on elephants even though a classmate made a not so nice comment and I wanted to stop. (5)
- I kept trying overhand serves in volleyball even when it was hard and even when they didn't go over the net. (3)
- I kept practicing multiplication facts even when I didn't want to and even when I got them wrong. (2)
- The first time I made a Ferris wheel, it didn't turn and I got frustrated. After I realized it needed a different piece, I got it to turn. (5)

Innovative (green)

- My watercolor painting got too watery, so I blotted it on another paper and it turned into a great background for a poem. (8)
- I made shoes out of cardboard and duct tape. (10)
- Swimming across the pool seemed like a big problem. My swim instructor helped me to focus on the stroke a different way. That helped my problem, and I swam across the pool. (11)
- One time, I made a remote-control car. (7)
- I love to draw! Especially dragons. (9)
- I create people out of different shapes and textures. (10)
- I dropped my completed Lego Jabba the Hut. I was really mad and sad. My mom helped me get all the pieces. The next day, I started remaking it. (7)
- I was trying to make a deer out of clay, but it turned out to look more like a fox, so I kept it. Then I tried making another deer. (8)
- I like to write different endings to fairy tales. (9)

Connecting (purple)

- I held my dog's paw when he got a shot at the vet. (12)
- I work together with my basketball team to make plays. (14)
- I listened to my sister tell all about her soccer tournament. (15)
- I helped clean up trash at school. (16)
- I helped my grandma rake the leaves at her house. (16)
- I helped a new student find the office and sat with her at lunch. (12)
- My mom and dad hug me all the time. (13)
- My teacher always smiles and tells us encouraging things in reading and math. (13)
- I listen to my friends when they are sad. (15)
- My group in science class worked together on an experiment. (14)

Additional (blue)

- Sometimes I feel like my fear of reading is a problem that will swallow me up. But I try each day to face it. (11)
- Questioner (20)
- Imaginer (20)
- Determined (19)
- Creative (19)
- Brave (19)

Key

- Resilient (orange)
- Innovative (green)
- Connecting (purple)
- Additional (blue)

Number in bubble indicates lesson number.

Rosie the Resilient

Part II

STRENGTH ONE : RESILIENT

Resilient: to keep going even when something is hard, even when you make mistakes, and even when you're afraid

> **Before beginning these lessons, have the following books on hand:**
> *Bubble Gum Brain: Ready, Get Mindset...Grow!* by Julia Cook
> *It's Okay to Make Mistakes* by Todd Parr
> *Trying* by Kobi Yamada
> *Rosie Revere, Engineer* by Andrea Beaty
> *The Don't Worry Book* by Todd Parr

Bubble Gum Brain by Julia Cook

Materials:
> Resilient Definition Card
> *Bubble Gum Brain: Ready, Get Mindset...Grow!* by Julia Cook
> optional prop: bubble gum
> students' Strengths Bubble Maps
> one orange marker for each student
> *Brilliantly Dyslexic* by Liz Trudeau

Definition: Show students the Resilient Definition Card and review the definition: Resilient means to to keep going even when something is hard, even when you make mistakes, and even when you're afraid.

Book Share: Read *Bubble Gum Brain: Ready, Get Mindset...Grow!* by Julia Cook. (Optional: Before reading the book as a class, hand out bubble gum to students.)

Discussion: Discuss as a class how the girl and boy are resilient. Write student responses on the board. Emphasize the power of making great mistakes and the power of "yet." Have students share about a time they were resilient or had to think of another way to do something. Choose from any of the following questions:
• Did you ever have to practice something a lot in order to be able to do it? (e.g., swimming across the pool, finishing a LEGO set)
• Is there a mistake that you've learned from? (e.g., when first serving a volleyball, hitting a baseball, building a LEGO set)
• Have you used "the power of yet"?
• What is an area where you'd like to use "the power of yet"?

Reflection: Write example strengths on the board as students share. Then write one to two examples of students' strengths on their Strengths Bubble Maps (or have students write it on their own or using speech-to-text in a Google Doc or Seesaw text page). Have students use an orange marker to bubble outline each recorded strength.

student

I kept practicing multi-plication facts even when I didn't want to and even when I got them wrong.

I am not good at layups in basketball—yet.

Brilliant People: Read about director **Steven Spielberg** in *Brilliantly Dyslexic* (pages 70–73) and discuss the ways he was resilient.

Extension: Choose any of the following activities to continue to explore the topic of resilience:

- Watch Quinn Bradlee, a student with dyslexia, interview Steven Spielberg:

  https://www.youtube.com/watch?v=-lGr840jE_0 (10:55)

- Watch an interview with actress Keira Knightly and discuss the ways she was resilient starting at six years old:

  https://www.youtube.com/watch?v=OLb6ehPPc4E (4:03)

- Read *Y Is for Yet: A Growth Mindset Alphabet* by Shannon Anderson, where students can discover letters like *C* is for Challenge, *P* is for Progress, and *R* is for Resilient.

- Read about another brilliant person, boxer **Ruqsana Begum**, in *Brilliantly Dyslexic* (pages 10–13) and discuss how she was resilient while becoming a European champion.

> **REMINDER**
>
> Share your own personal experiences with being resilient with your students/children.

It's Okay to Make Mistakes by Todd Parr

Materials:
> Resilient Definition Card
> *It's Okay to Make Mistakes* by Todd Parr
> students' Strengths Bubble Maps
> one orange marker for each student
> *Brilliantly Dyslexic* by Liz Trudeau

Definition: Show students the Resilient Definition Card and review the definition: Resilient means to keep going even when something is hard, even when you make mistakes, and even when you're afraid.

Book Share: Read *It's Okay to Make Mistakes* by Todd Parr.

Discussion: Have students share about a time they made a mistake and kept trying. Choose from any of the following questions:

• Has there been a time when you were drawing or painting and kept making mistakes?

• Was there a time you tried a new dance or sports move and made a mistake but kept going?

• What encourages you or who encourages you when you make a mistake?

Reflection: Write example strengths on the board as students share. Then write one to two examples of students' strengths on their Strengths Bubble Maps (or have students write it on their own or using speech-to-text in a Google Doc or Seesaw text page). Have students use an orange marker to bubble outline each recorded strength.

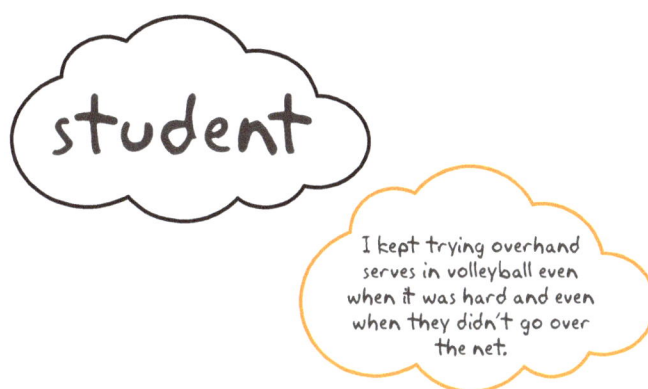

Brilliant People: Read the biography of entrepreneur **Cliff Weitzman** in *Brilliantly Dyslexic* (pages 78–81) and discuss the ways he was resilient.

Extension: Choose any of the following activities to continue to explore the topic of resilience:

- Download the Speechify app and have students practice reading text in Google Docs or Gmail with it: https://speechify.com/
- Read *Where the Red Fern Grows* by Wilson Rawls aloud to the class. Alternatively, encourage students to add *Where the Red Fern Grows* to their audiobooks or Learning Ally bookshelf. After reading the book, discuss as a class how Billy was resilient.
- Read about *Mistakes That Worked: The World's Familiar Inventions and How They Came to Be* by Charlotte Foltz Jones.

Trying by Kobi Yamada

Materials:
> Resilient Definition Card
> *Trying* by Kobi Yamada
> students' Strengths Bubble Maps
> one orange marker for each student
> *Brilliantly Dyslexic* by Liz Trudeau

Definition: Show students the Resilient Definition Card and review the definition: Resilient means to keep going even when something is hard, even when you make mistakes, and even when you're afraid.

Book Share: Read *Trying* by Kobi Yamada.

Discussion: Have students share about a time they were resilient.[1] Choose from any of the following questions:
• Share about a time that you had a failure that helped you learn.
• Who encourages you to keep trying?
• At the end of the book, the sculptor shows the statues and says, "These are my friends. These are my failures." What does that mean?

Reflection: Write example strengths on the board as students share. Then write one to two examples of students' strengths on their Strengths Bubble Maps (or have students write it on their own or using speech-to-text in a Google Doc or Seesaw text page). Have students use an orange marker to bubble outline each recorded strength.

---

1 If students have difficulty coming up with additional examples, try not to pressure them for more. Affirm the ones they already recorded on their Strengths Bubble Maps, and ask again tomorrow. Some students just need more time to think about it.

student

> I got frustrated when I kept making mistakes on my paintings. Some of them didn't turn out like I wanted. But I made the adjustments and finished one that was just right.

Brilliant People: Read the biography of entrepreneur **Richard Branson** in *Brilliantly Dyslexic* (pages 18–21) and discuss the ways he was resilient.

Extension: Choose any of the following activities to continue to explore the topic of resilience.

- Watch an interview with Richard Branson:

  https://www.youtube.com/watch?v=-OZyXZ__5TU (4:33)

- Watch an interview with Charles Schwab, another successful businessman with dyslexia:

  https://www.youtube.com/watch?v=ZLHQPRCCkcs (10:02)

- Read a biography about Nelson Rockefeller, former vice president with dyslexia:

  http://dyslexiahelp.umich.edu/success-stories/nelson-rockefeller

- Read about **David Hornik**, a venture capitalist, in *Brilliantly Dyslexic* (pages 42–45).

HELPFUL HINT

If students are having difficulty thinking of a personal example, share your observations of them being resilient.

Rosie Revere, Engineer by Andrea Beaty

Materials:
> Resilient Definition Card
> *Rosie Revere, Engineer* by Andrea Beaty
> students' Strengths Bubble Maps
> one orange marker for each student
> *Brilliantly Dyslexic* by Liz Trudeau

Definition: Show students the Resilient Definition Card and review the definition: Resilient means to keep going even when something is hard, even when you make mistakes, and even when you're afraid.

Book Share: Read *Rosie Revere, Engineer* by Andrea Beaty.

Discussion: Have students share about a time they were resilient. Choose from any of the following questions:
• What is something you have created or invented?
• Rosie's Uncle Fred laughed at her invention, and she stopped. Has there been a time someone laughed at your creation/invention and you stopped?
• Great-Great-Aunt Rose laughed too. Rosie almost stopped but didn't. Is there a time someone has laughed or made a comment about something you were creating and you kept trying?

Reflection: Write example strengths on the board as students share. Then write one to two examples of students' strengths on their Strengths Bubble Maps (or have students write it on their own or using speech-to-text in a Google Doc or Seesaw text page). Have students use an orange marker to bubble outline each recorded strength.

student

I kept writing the report on elephants even though a classmate made a not so nice comment and I wanted to stop.

The first time I made a Ferris wheel, it didn't turn and I got frustrated. After I realized it needed a different piece, I got it to turn.

Brilliant People: Read the biography of space scientist **Maggie Aderin-Pocock** in *Brilliantly Dyslexic* (pages 2–5) and discuss the ways that she was resilient.

Extension: Choose any of the following activities to continue to explore the topic of resilience:

- Learn more about telescopes:
  - Use a telescope to look at the stars and planets.
  - Download a telescope app such as SkyView and discover the constellations.
  - Visit your local planetarium.
  - Read *Telescopes for Kids: A Junior Scientist's Guide to Stargazing, Constellations, and Discovering Far Off Galaxies* by Vanessa Thomas.
- Give students a bag of various LEGOs, pipe cleaners, nuts, screws, etc., and see what they invent.
- Read books about inventors like Leonardo da Vinci, Thomas Alva Edison, Nikola Tesla, and more in the Who Was? series.
- Read about more innovators in *Spectacular Stories for Curious Kids* by Jessie Sullivan.

BRILLIANT FACT

Brilliant Fact: It took Thomas Edison 1,000 tries to invent the lightbulb. He is noted as saying, "I didn't fail 1,000 times. The lightbulb was an invention with 1,000 steps."

The Don't Worry Book by Todd Parr

Materials:
> Resilient Definition Card
> *The Don't Worry Book* by Todd Parr
> students' Strengths Bubble Maps
> one orange marker for each student
> *Brilliantly Dyslexic* by Liz Trudeau

Definition: Show students the Resilient Definition Card and review the definition: Resilient means to keep going even when something is hard, even when you make mistakes, and even when you're afraid.

Book Share: Read *The Don't Worry Book* by Todd Parr.

Discussion: Have students share about a time they were resilient when feeling worried or afraid. Choose from any of the following questions:

• Tell us about a time you felt afraid.

• Was there a time when you were worried and you did something anyway? (e.g., raise your hand in class, share an idea, say your opinion)

• Near the end of the book, Todd Parr provides helpful strategies to use when you're worried. Which ones have you used? Which ones would you like to try?

Reflection: Write example strengths on the board as students share. Then write one to two examples of students' strengths on their Strengths Bubble Maps (or have students write it on their own or using speech-to-text in a Google Doc or Seesaw text page). Have students use an orange marker to bubble outline each recorded strength.

student

In math class I was scared, but I raised my hand to answer a question.

I competed in my first swim meet even though I was really afraid.

Brilliant People: Read the biography of principal ballerina **Darcey Bussell** in *Brilliantly Dyslexic* (pages 22–25) and discuss the ways Darcey was resilient even when she was afraid.

Extension: Choose any of the following activities to continue to explore the topic of resilience:

- As a read aloud, read *Fish in a Tree* by Lynda Mullaly Hunt. After reading the book, discuss how Ally, a student with dyslexia, is resilient even when afraid.
- Watch the movie *Luca* (1:35:00), focusing on the scene when Alberto introduces the phrase "Silenzio Bruno!" (In this scene, Alberto tells Luca to say "Silenzio Bruno" to encourage him to overcome his inner "Bruno," his fears and worries. Discuss the meaning of the phrase and how students can relate to it.)
- Watch the movie *Leap* (1:29:00), noting the ways that Felicie is resilient when auditioning for the Grand Opera House in Paris.
- Hear Darcey Bussell share about her journey with dyslexia and how important it is to focus on strengths: https://www.youtube.com/watch?v=_6tRLwR2QEs (3:25)
- Read additional books about worry and fear:
  - *Wilma Jean the Worry Machine* by Julia Cook
  - *Courage* by Bernard Waber
  - *What to Do When You Worry Too Much: A Kid's Guide to Overcoming Anxiety* by Dawn Huebner

SPECIAL NOTE

Students can often mask their worries and fears. This lesson is an opportunity for them to name their fears and worries. It also provides tools to help them in various situations.

Ivan the Innovator

Part III

STRENGTH TWO : INNOVATIVE

Innovative: to create, invent, and see things in a different way: "to think outside the box"

> **Before beginning these lessons, have the following books on hand:**

The Most Magnificent Thing by Ashley Spires

Beautiful Oops! by Barney Saltzberg or

The Book of Mistakes by Corinna Luyken

The Pencil by Allan Ahlberg

What If… by Samantha Berger

What Do You Do with a Problem? by Kobi Yamada

The Most Magnificent Thing by Ashley Spires

Materials:
> Innovative Definition Card
> *The Most Magnificent Thing* by Ashley Spires
> students' Strengths Bubble Maps
> one green marker for each student
> *Brilliantly Dyslexic* by Liz Trudeau

Definition: Show students the Innovative Definition Card and review the definition: Innovative means to create, invent, and see things in a different way; to "think outside the box."

Book Share: Read *The Most Magnificent Thing* by Ashley Spires.

Discussion: Have students share about a time they were innovative. Choose from any of the following questions:
• Tell us about one of your inventions or creations.
• Has there been a time when you were making something and you got really, really frustrated, and you didn't feel like going on?
• Who or what encourages you when you don't feel like continuing a creation or invention?
• Have you ever dropped an invention or creation and had to rebuild it?
• Has there been a time when you were building or drawing something and it ended up turning into something else?

Reflection: Write example strengths on the board as students share. Then write one to two examples of students' strengths on their Strengths Bubble Maps (or have students write it on their own or using speech-to-text in a Google Doc or Seesaw text page). Have students use a green marker to bubble outline each recorded strength.

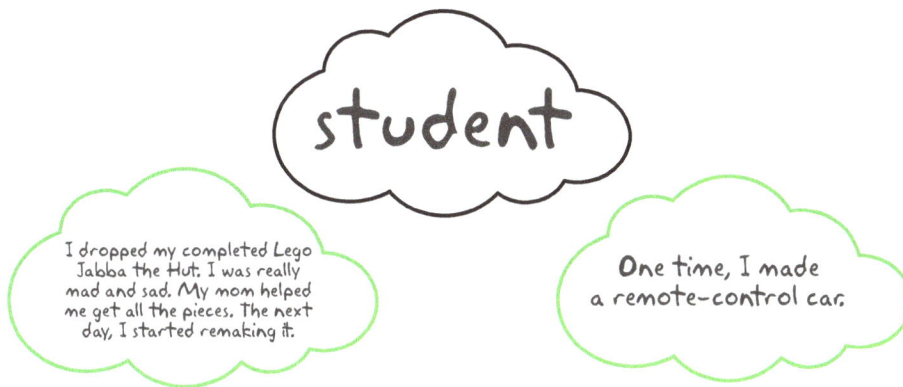

student

I dropped my completed Lego Jabba the Hut. I was really mad and sad. My mom helped me get all the pieces. The next day, I started remaking it.

One time, I made a remote-control car.

Brilliant People: Read the biography of software engineer **Maria Naggaga** in *Brilliantly Dyslexic* (pages 54–57) and discuss the ways she was innovative.

Extension: Choose any of the following activities to continue to explore the topic of innovation.

- Download the following apps for students who have an interest in mazes or coding: AMAZE! (12 and up), codeSpark Academy (ages 4–9), ScratchJr (ages 5–7), Scratch (ages 8–16), Mimo app (ages 12 and up).
- Watch an interview with Maria Naggaga about interactive learning and coding: https://docs.microsoft.com/en-us/shows/On-NET/Maria-Naggaga-Interactive-learning-with-Try-NET (12:56)[1]

SPECIAL NOTE

This lesson and resources are especially helpful for students who have difficulty identifying their emotions and/or regulating their emotions.

---

1 This interview is geared towards students who have some background understanding of coding.

- Read about more innovators like Walt Disney, Bill Gates, the Wright Brothers, and Maria Montessori in *Kid Innovators: True Tales of Childhood from Inventors and Trailblazers* by Robin Stevenson.
- Read about Jack Horner, paleontologist and professor with dyslexia: http://dyslexiahelp.umich.edu/success-stories/jack-horner
- Put wires, screws, pipe cleaners, duct tape, and cardboard in a bag, and have students create something.
- Use your imagination and play the games found in the book *The Floor Is Lava: And 99 More Games for Everyone, Everywhere* by teacher Ivan Brett.
- The girl in *The Most Magnificent Thing* experiences several emotions. Explore emotions more by reading any of the following books:
  - *The Way I Feel* by Janan Cain
  - *My Many Colored Days* by Dr. Seuss
  - *ABC Book of Feelings* by Marlys Boddy
  - *In My Heart: A Book of Feeling*s by Jo Witek
  - The Emotional Impact series by Adolph Moser, illustrated by Dav Pilkey:
    Don't Pop Your Cork on Mondays!
      The Children's Anti-Stress Book
    Don't Feed the Monster on Tuesdays!
      The Children's Self-Esteem Book
    Don't Rant and Rave on Wednesdays!
      The Children's Anger-Control Book
    Don't Despair on Thursdays!
      The Children's Grief-Management Book

Extension for Teachers and Parents: If your student has big emotions or big reactions, use the following resources to further explore emotional regulation:

- *The Zones of Regulation™* by Leah Kuypers
- *Superflex Takes on Glassman and the Team of Unthinkables*, part of the Social Thinking™ curriculum by Michelle Garcia Winner
- Executive Functions "Emotibot: Emotional Control," the character used to describe emotional control on the website EFs 2 the Rescue: http://efs2therescue.com/emotibot-emotional-control
- *Executive Function 101* by National Center for Learning Disabilities: https://www.chconline.org/resourcelibrary/executive-function-101-e-book-downloadable/

Beautiful Oops! by Barney Saltzberg or
The Book of Mistakes by Corinna Luyken

Materials:

> Innovative Definition Card

> *Beautiful Oops!* by Barnie Saltzberg (younger students) or
   The Book of Mistakes by Corinna Luyken (older students)

> students' Strengths Bubble Maps

> one green marker for each student

> *Brilliantly Dyslexic* by Liz Trudeau

Definition: Show students the Innovative Definition Card and review the definition: Innovative means to create, invent, and see things in a different way; to "think outside the box."

Book Share: Read *Beautiful Oops!* by Barney Saltzberg or *The Book of Mistakes* by Corinna Luyken.

Discussion: Have students share about a time they were innovative and they made something out of an "oops" moment or a mistake. Choose from any of the following questions:

• In *Beautiful Oops!* and in *The Book of Mistakes*, many "oops" moments occur, and the mistake turns into something else. Has there been a time when you were making something and you ended up turning it into something else? What was it?

• When you have an "oops" moment, what can help remind you that it is an opportunity to make something beautiful?

• Tell us about something you created out of paper, paint, ink, or newspaper.

Reflection: Write example strengths on the board as students share. Then write one to two examples of students' strengths on their Strengths Bubble Maps (or have students write it on their own or using speech-to-text in a Google Doc or Seesaw text page). Have students use a green marker to bubble outline each recorded strength.

student

My watercolor painting got too watery, so I blotted it on another paper and it turned into a great background for a poem.

I was trying to make a deer out of clay, but it turned out to look more like a fox, so I kept it. Then I tried making another deer.

Brilliant People: Read the biography of pastry chef **Elisabeth Prueitt** in *Brilliantly Dyslexic* (pages 62–65) and discuss how she was innovative.

Extension:

- Bake a treat from one of Elisabeth Prueitt's cookbooks like *Tartine All Day: Modern Recipes for the Home Cook*, from a children's cookbook like *Bake Up! Kids Cookbook: Go from Beginner to Pro with 60 Recipes & Essential Techniques* by Nicole Hendizadeh, or from one of your favorite family recipes.
- In pairs, have each partner draw a random line, squiggle, or design on a piece of paper. Have the partners trade papers and turn their partner's line, squiggle, or design into a drawing of something new.
- Read about how **Vernon François**, a hair stylist, is innovative in *Brilliantly Dyslexic* (pages 34–37).

> ## REMINDER
>
> Share your own personal experiences with being innovative with your students.

The Pencil by Allan Ahlberg

Materials:
> Innovative Definition Card
> *The Pencil* by Allan Ahlberg
> students' Strengths Bubble Maps
> one green marker for each student
> *Brilliantly Dyslexic* by Liz Trudeau

Definition: Show students the Innovative Definition Card and review the definition: Innovative means to create, invent, and see things in a different way; to "think outside the box."

Book Share: Read *The Pencil* by Allan Ahlberg.

Discussion: Have students share about a time they were innovative and had to see things in a different way. Choose from any of the following questions:
- *The Pencil* is a creative story with creative illustrations. Tell us about a creative story you have written or illustrated.
- The big eraser is used to transform the character's details. Do you have a big eraser for making changes?
- How was the author innovative throughout *The Pencil*?

Reflection: Write example strengths on the board as students share. Then write one to two examples of students' strengths on their Strengths Bubble Maps (or have students write it on their own or using speech-to-text in a Google Doc or Seesaw text page). Have students use a green marker to bubble outline each recorded strength.

student

I love to draw! Especially dragons.

I like to write different endings to fairy tales.

Brilliant People: Read the biography of shoe designer **John Hoke** in *Brilliantly Dyslexic* (pages 38–41) and discuss how he was innovative.

Extension: Choose any of the following activities to continue to explore the topic of innovation:

- Read aloud any of the following "think outside the box" mysteries and discuss how the authors see things differently.
  - Spy School series by Stuart Gibbs
  - Ballpark Mysteries series by David A. Kelly
  - *If You're Reading This, It's Too Late* by Pseudonymous Bosch
  - *Escape From Mr. Lemoncello's Library* by Chris Grabenstein
  - *The Body Under the Piano* by Marthe Jocelyn
  - *Charlie & Frog: A Mystery* by Karen Kane
  - *Clubhouse Mysteries: Lost in the Tunnel of Time* by Sharon M. Draper
  - *Case Closed #1: Mystery in the Mansion* by Lauren Magaziner
  - Agatha Christie mysteries such as *And Then There Were None* (for older students)
- Solve the mysteries in the game Cat Crimes.
- Read *Ish* by Peter Reynoles and discuss how Ramon is innovative and resilient.
- Read about how software engineer **Dona Sarkar** thinks outside the box in *Brilliantly Dyslexic* (pages 66–69).

BRILLIANT FACT

Undeterred by dysgraphia (a neurological disorder that primarily affects handwriting and can also affect spelling and written expression), Agatha Christie went on to author mysteries and short stories that have sold over four billion copies.

What If... by Samantha Berger

Materials:
> Innovative Definition Card
> *What If...* by Samantha Berger
> students' Strengths Bubble Maps
> one green marker for each student
> *Brilliantly Dyslexic* by Liz Trudeau

Definition: Show students the Innovative Definition Card and review the definition: Innovative means to create, invent, and see things in a different way; to "think outside the box."

Book Share: Read *What If...* by Samantha Berger.

Discussion: Have students share about a time they created something out of paper, wood or paint, or using their voice or body. Choose from any of the following questions:
• Tell us about something you made out of pencil, paper, paint, clay, wood, sand, or snow.
• Have you ever made up a song? What was the song about?
• Tell us about a dance or a sports move you've created.

Reflection: Write example strengths on the board as students share. Then write one to two examples of students' strengths on their Strengths Bubble Maps (or have students write it on their own or using speech-to-text in a Google Doc or Seesaw text page). Have students use a green marker to bubble outline each recorded strength.

student

I create people out of different shapes and textures.

I made shoes out of cardboard and duct tape.

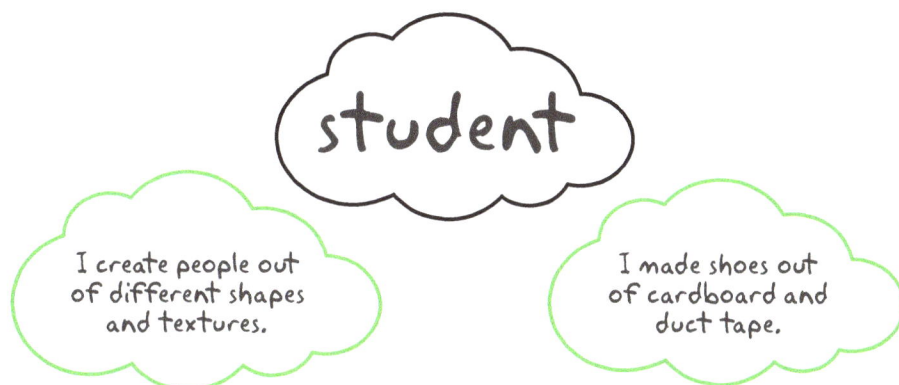

Brilliant People: Read the biography of artist **Heather Day** in *Brilliantly Dyslexic* (pages 26–29) and discuss how she was innovative.

Extension: Choose any of the following activities to continue to explore the topic of innovation:

- Learn about how author Eric Carle created his "picture writings": https://www.youtube.com/watch?v=S0INNN6jh74 (32:07)

- Provide students with paint, construction paper, wood, glitter, beads, buttons, snow, and sand for them to create something new.

- Encourage students to read about other artists in the following books:

  - *Linnea in Monet's Garden* by Christina Bjork
  - *Grandpa and the Library: How Charles White Learned to Paint* by C. Ian White
  - *Frida Kahlo and Her Animalitos* by Monica Brown

HELPFUL HINT

If students are having difficulty thinking of a personal example, share your observations of them being innovative.

What Do You Do with a Problem? by Kobi Yamada

Materials:
> Innovative Definition Card
> *What Do You Do with a Problem?* by Kobi Yamada
> students' Strengths Bubble Maps
> one green marker for each student
> *Brilliantly Dyslexic* by Liz Trudeau

Definition: Show students the Innovative Definition Card and review the definition: Innovative means to create, invent, and see things in a different way; to "think outside the box."

Book Share: Read *What Do You Do with a Problem?* by Kobi Yamada.

Discussion: Have students share about a time they have had a problem and how they viewed it or faced it.
• Throughout the book, the boy is worried about the problem that appears, and he feels like the problem will swallow him up. Has there been a time when you were worried about a problem? What was it?
• How does the boy start to think of the problem differently? What does he do? When you faced a problem, were you able to think of the problem differently?
• At the end of the book, how does the boy see things differently?
• What can you do the next time you have a problem?

Reflection: Write example strengths on the board as students share. Then write one to two examples of students' strengths on their Strengths Bubble Maps (or have students write it on their own or using speech-to-text in a Google Doc or Seesaw text page). Have students use a green marker to bubble outline each recorded strength.

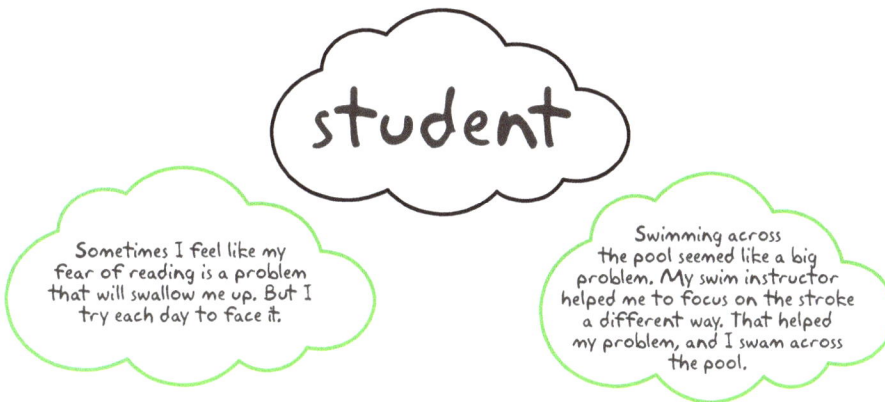

student

Sometimes I feel like my fear of reading is a problem that will swallow me up. But I try each day to face it.

Swimming across the pool seemed like a big problem. My swim instructor helped me to focus on the stroke a different way. That helped my problem, and I swam across the pool.

Brilliant People: Read the biography of doctor **Beryl Benacerraf** in *Brilliantly Dyslexic* (pages 14–17) and discuss how she had a different perspective.

Extension: Choose any of the following activities to continue to explore the topic of innovation:

- Read books about problem solving. Seeing the bigger picture can help us solve problems, and many books show the process of problem solving. Check out the following graphic novels and see how the problems are solved.
- For younger students:
  - *Captain Underpants* series by Dav Pilkey
  - *Dog Man* series by Dav Pilkey
  - *Elephant & Piggie* series by Mo Willems
  - *The Pigeon* series by Mo Willems
  - *Narwhal and Jelly* series by Ben Clanton

BRILLIANT FACT

It took Dav Pilkey twenty-four tries to get his first book published.

- For older students:
  - *Big Nate* series by Lincoln Peirce
  - *Phoebe and Her Unicorn* series by Dana Simpson
  - *Diary of a Wimpy Kid* series by Jeff Kinney
  - *Sunny Side Up* series by Jennifer L. Holm
  - *New Kid* by Jerry Craft
- Learn more about the creator and author of *Captain Underpants* and *Dog Man*, Dav Pilkey, who has dyslexia.
  - Learn about Dav's struggles with reading in this interview by kid reporter William Russell: https://www.youtube.com/watch?v=be1l4y-eflY (1:15)
  - Create graphics like Dav Pilkey: https://www.youtube.com/watch?v=Y5MgYqkvuwM (3:09)
  - Put this interview with Dav Pilkey in your parent newsletter: https://www.scholastic.com/parents/family-life/parent-child/qa-captain-underpants-author-dav-pilkey.html
  - Use these "Free Printable Comic Book Templates" to create your own graphic novel: https://picklebums.com/free-printable-comic-book-templates/

Carl the Connector

Part IV

STRENGTH THREE : CONNECTING

Connecting: to show kindness, to work together, and to communicate well with others

> **Before beginning these lessons, have the following books on hand:**
>
> *What Does It Mean to Be Kind?* by Rana DiOrio
>
> *Thank You, Mr. Falker* by Patricia Polacco
>
> *Up the Creek* by Nicholas Oldland
>
> *Why Should I Listen?* by Claire Llewellyn
>
> *Sofia Valdez, Future Prez* by Andrea Beaty

What Does It Mean to Be Kind? by Rain DiOrio

Materials:
> Connecting Definition Card
> *What Does It Mean to Be Kind?* by Rana DiOrio
> students' Strengths Bubble Maps
> one purple marker for each student
> *Brilliantly Dyslexic* by Liz Trudeau

Definition: Show students the Connecting Definition Card and review the definition: Connecting means to show kindness, to work together, and to communicate well with others.

Book Share: Read *What Does It Mean to Be Kind?* by Rana DiOrio.

Discussion: Have students share about a time they showed kindness. Choose from any of the following prompts:
• Describe a time when you were kind…
  - welcoming someone new
  - encouraging someone with kind words
  - sticking up for someone
  - forgiving someone
  - being patient with your family members or friends
  - using polite manners
  - helping an injured animal

Reflection: Write example strengths on the board as students share. Then write one to two examples of students' strengths on their Strengths Bubble Maps (or have students write it on their own or using speech-to-text in a Google Doc or Seesaw text page). Have students use a purple marker to bubble outline each recorded strength.

student

I helped a new student find the office and sat with her at lunch.

I held my dog's paw when he got a shot at the vet.

Brilliant People: Read the biography of behavioral ecologist **Kate Evans** in *Brilliantly Dyslexic* (pages 30–34) and discuss the ways that she shows kindness to elephants.

Extension: Choose any of the following activities to continue to explore the topic of connection.

- As a class, read *Wonder* by R. J. Palacio or *Royal Bee* by Frances and Ginger Park (or have students add it to their Learning Ally or audiobook list). After reading the book, discuss how the characters show kindness to one another.

- Read *The Elephant's New Shoe* by Laurel Neme or watch the movie *Dolphin Tale* (1:54:00) and discuss the following:
  - how people show kindness to animals
  - how the accommodations for the animals helped them
  - your accommodations and how they have helped you

- Read about writer and professor **Ocean Vuong** in *Brilliantly Dyslexic* (pages 74–77) and how he uses words to connect to others.

SPECIAL NOTE

This lesson is a good opportunity to review accommodations with your students to make sure that 1) they are aware of their specific accommodations and 2) they advocate for and use their accommodations in class. Sometimes students do not want to "stand out" in their classes and do not use their accommodations. If this is the case, talk with the student and teacher about a non-verbal signal that can be used or any helpful tool they feel comfortable using.

Thank You, Mr. Falker by Patricia Polacco

Materials:

> Connecting Definition Card
> *Thank you, Mr. Falker* by Patricia Polacco
> students' Strengths Bubble Maps
> one purple marker for each student
> *Brilliantly Dyslexic* by Liz Trudeau

Definition: Show students the Connecting Definition Card and review the definition: Connecting means to show kindness, to work together, and to communicate well with others.

Book Share: Read *Thank You, Mr. Falker* by Patricia Polacco.

Discussion: Have students share about a time a parent, grandparent, or teacher showed kindness to them. Choose from any of the following prompts:

• Describe a time your parent or grandparent showed kindness to you.

• How has a teacher shown kindness to you in the classroom?

• Mr. Falker shows kindness to Patty and her classmates. How have you shown kindness to your classmates at school?

• What actions and words could you use to show kindness to your friends and classmates?

Reflection: Write example strengths on the board as students share. Then write one to two examples of students' strengths on their Strengths Bubble Maps (or have students write it on their own or using speech-to-text in a Google Doc or Seesaw text page). Have students use a purple marker to bubble outline each recorded strength.

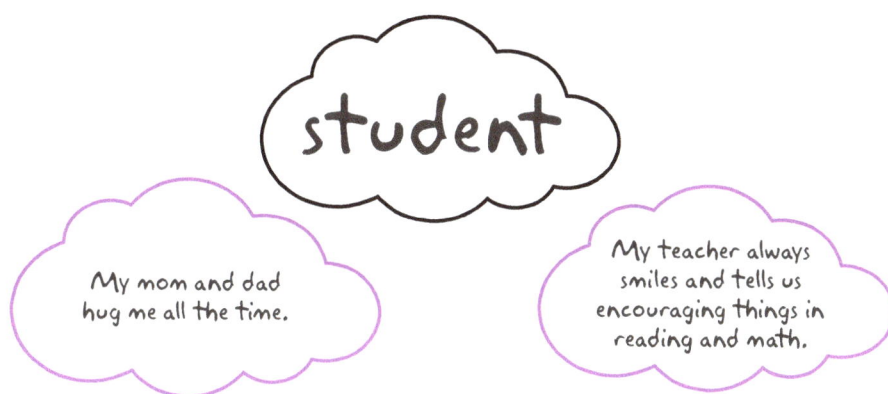

student

My mom and dad hug me all the time.

My teacher always smiles and tells us encouraging things in reading and math.

Brilliant People: Read the biography of polar explorer **Ann Bancroft** in *Brilliantly Dyslexic* (pages 6–9) and discuss how she and her students and staff showed kindness toward each other.

Extension: Choose any of the following activities to continue to explore the topic of connection:

- Watch this interview with Patricia Palocco, an author with dyslexia, and learn about her journey with dyslexia and how the original Mr. Falker changed her life: https://www.youtube.com/watch?v=4uxlMV8uJAs (1:58)
- Write a thank you note to someone who has been kind to you.
- Continue to read about kindness in *The Invisible Boy* by Trudy Ludwig or *The Kindness Book* by Todd Parr.

Up the Creek by Nicholas Oldland

Materials:
> Connecting Definition Card
> *Up the Creek* by Nicholas Oldland
> students' Strengths Bubble Maps
> one purple marker for each student
> *Brilliantly Dyslexic* by Liz Trudeau

Definition: Show students the Connecting Definition Card and review the definition: Connecting means to show kindness, to work together, and to communicate well with others.

Book Share: Read *Up the Creek* by Nicholas Oldland.

Discussion: Have students share about a time they had to work together with someone or a team. Choose from any of the following prompts:
• When have you worked with someone on a project? (e.g., at school, on a sports team, on a debate team, in the band or orchestra)
• Have you disagreed with someone you were working with? What helped you find a way to work together?

Reflection: Write example strengths on the board as students share. Then write one to two examples of students' strengths on their Strengths Bubble Maps (or have students write it on their own or using speech-to-text in a Google Doc or Seesaw text page). Have students use a purple marker to bubble outline each recorded strength.

student

I work together with my basketball team to make plays.

My group in science class worked together on an experiment.

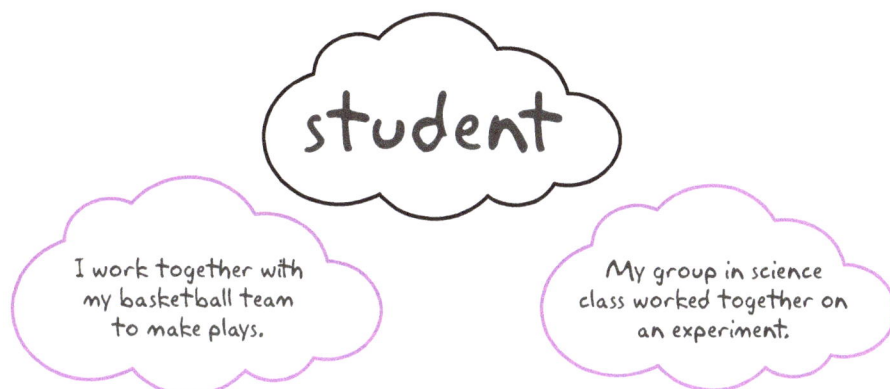

Brilliant People: Read the biography of NFL coach **Joe Whitt Jr.** in *Brilliantly Dyslexic* (pages 82–85) and discuss how he worked together with his team and with other coaches.

Extension: Choose any of the following activities to continue to explore the topic of connection:

- Working together is important, especially in team sports. Read about other athletes with dyslexia:
  - Olympian rower Steve Redgrave: http://dyslexiahelp.umich.edu/steve-redgrave
  - Major League Baseball player Nolan Ryan: http://dyslexiahelp.umich.edu/success-stories/nolan-ryan
  - NFL football player Tim Tebow: http://dyslexiahelp.umich.edu/success-stories/tim-tebow
- Read about your favorite sports figures in these book series:
  - *Amazing Athletes* by various authors
  - *Victory School Superstars* by various authors
  - *Comeback Kids* by Mike Lupica
  - *Middle School Rules* by Sean Jensen
- Read the biography of basketball player **Magic Johnson** in *Brilliantly Dyslexic* (pages 46–49) and discuss how he not only shows the strength of resilience but also works together with his team.

Why Should I Listen? by Claire Llewellyn

Materials:
> Connecting Definition Card
> *Why Should I Listen?* by Claire Llewellyn
> students' Strengths Bubble Maps
> one purple marker for each student
> *Brilliantly Dyslexic* by Liz Trudeau

Definition: Show students the Connecting Definition Card and review the definition: Connecting means to show kindness, to work together, and to communicate well with others.

Book Share: Read *Why Should I Listen?* by Claire Llewellyn.

Discussion: Have students share about a time they listened or did not listen well.

- Do you listen to your family during dinner or your friends while eating lunch with them?
- Describe a time when a family member or friend had something exciting to share or a problem to share and you listened.
- Have you ever had something important to say and the other person wasn't listening? How did it feel?

Reflection: Write example strengths on the board as students share. Then write one to two examples of students' strengths on their Strengths Bubble Maps (or have students write it on their own or using speech-to-text in a Google Doc or Seesaw text page). Have students use a purple marker to bubble outline each recorded strength.

student

I listen to my friends when they are sad.

I listened to my sister tell all about her soccer tournament.

Brilliant People: Read the biography of journalist **Byron Pitts** in *Brilliantly Dyslexic* (pages 58–61) and share how his struggle learning to read led to his listening to and connecting with some of the world's greatest leaders.

Extension: Choose any of the following activities to continue to explore the topic of connection:

- Telling stories and listening to them is a fun way to communicate. Silly stories and jokes are a lot of fun! Read jokes from a joke book like *Knock Knock Jokes for Funny Kids* by Jimmy Jones or *Laugh-Out-Loud: The 1,001 Funniest LOL Jokes of All Times* by Rob Elliott.

- Listen to the great storyteller comedians Jay Leno and Whoopi Goldberg share not only their jokes but also their journey with dyslexia:
  - *Dyslexia and What I Would Tell #MyYoungerSelf: Jay Leno* https://www.youtube.com/watch?v=gkFPsFVo7zw (0:58)
  - *Founder Quinn Bradlee Talks Dyslexia with Whoopi Goldberg* https://www.youtube.com/watch?v=IMBDPOXbAHo (5:12)

- Play the game Telephone[1] to test out your students' listening skills, or go to the website Gartic Phone (https://garticphone. com) to create a game, send a link, and have others join.

> **REMINDER**
>
> Share your own personal experiences with being connecting with your students.

---

1 To play Telephone, have everyone sit in a circle. Choose one person to be the "telephone." The telephone person must think of a phrase to say, for example, "I like to eat peanut butter and jelly sandwiches with bananas." They then whisper the phrase to the next person in the circle. That person then whispers it to the next person. The last person to hear the phrase says it out loud. Discuss with the group: Was the phrase the same? Or did it turn into something else? How did it change? What was difficult about playing this game?

Sofia Valdez, Future Prez by Andrea Beaty

Materials:
> Connecting Definition Card
> *Sofia Valdez, Future Prez* by Andrea Beaty
> students' Strengths Bubble Maps
> one purple marker for each student
> *Brilliantly Dyslexic* by Liz Trudeau

Definition: Show students the Connecting Definition Card and review the definition: Connecting means to show kindness, to work together, and to communicate well with others.

Book Share: Read *Sofia Valdez, Future Prez* by Andrea Beaty.

Discussion: Have students share about a time they helped a family member, friend, or someone in their community. Choose from any of the following prompts:
• How do you help your parents or grandparents in your home?
• Has there been a time when you helped clean or build something in your neighborhood or school?
• Sofia is a leader. Share about a time that you led a group, a team, or a project.

Reflection: Write example strengths on the board as students share. Then write one to two examples of students' strengths on their Strengths Bubble Maps (or have students write it on their own or using speech-to-text in a Google Doc or Seesaw text page). Have students use a purple marker to bubble outline each recorded strength.

student

I helped clean up trash at school.

I helped my grandma rake the leaves at her house.

Brilliant People: Read the biography of politician and diplomat **Carol Moseley Braun** in *Brilliantly Dyslexic* (pages 50–53) and discuss the ways she works with others for change.

Extension: Choose any of the following activities to continue to explore the topic of connection:

- Hear how HRH Princess Beatrice works with others to raise dyslexia awareness and how she uses her job to communicate with others:
  https://www.youtube.com/watch?v=JrSV-rLaVCA (3:39)
- Read *Acts of Kindness* by Melissa Cenatiempo and learn how one simple act of kindness can spread to many.
- Discover how a city in Texas started a painted rock trail during the COVID-19 pandemic and how it grew through the community and beyond: https://www.dallasnews.com/arts-entertainment/lifestyle/2020/10/16/new-tourist-attraction-in-grapevine-started-as-act-of-kindness-during-covid-19-pandemic/
- Have students paint rocks of their own and find a special place to put them.
- Read more about kindness and passing it on in *Will You Be the "I" in Kind?* by Julia Cook.
- Read about activist **Joshua Wong** in *Brilliantly Dyslexic* (pages 86–89) and how he worked with others to have their voices heard.

HELPFUL HINT

If students are having difficulty thinking of a personal example, share your observations of them being connecting.

Rosie the Resilient

Resilient: to keep going even when something is hard, even when you make mistakes, and even when you're afraid

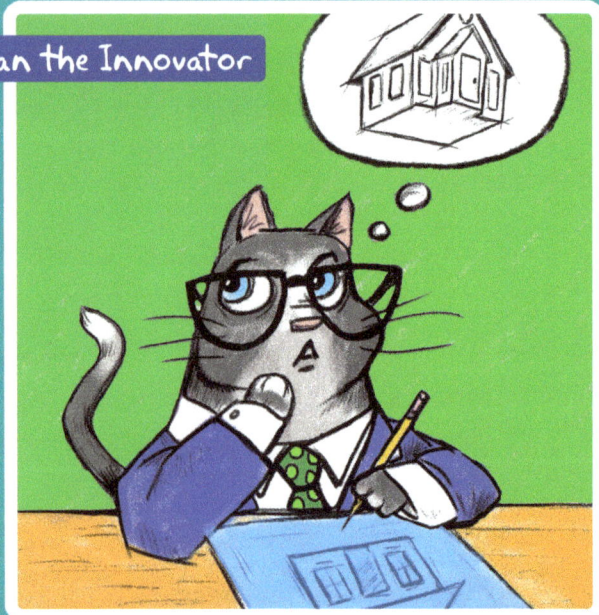
Ivan the Innovator

Innovative: to create, invent, and see things in a different way; to "think outside the box"

Carl the Connector

Connecting: to show kindness, to work together, and to communicate well with others

Part V

CELEBRATION : CELEBRATE STUDENT STRENGTHS AND ENGAGEMENT IN READING

**❯ Before beginning these lessons,
have the following books on hand:**

I Knew You Could!: A Book for All the Stops in Your Life
by Craig Dorfman
What the Road Said by Cleo Wade
Just Read! by Lori Degman

I Knew You Could! by Craig Dorfman or
What the Road Said by Cleo Wade

Materials:
> streamers and/or balloons, a bag with cupcakes/cookies, confetti, toy train or car (optional)
> Definition Cards (Resilient, Innovative, Connecting)
> *I Knew You Could! A Book for All the Stops in Your Life* by Craig Dorfman or *What the Road Said* by Cleo Wade
> color copies of students' Strengths Bubble Maps
> *Brilliantly Dyslexic* by Liz Trudeau

Introduction: Decorate your classroom or learning space with streamers and/or balloons. Place the following items in a bag: cupcakes/cookies, confetti, toy train or car. Have a student pull the items out of the bag. Tell students that it is a celebration day: It is a day to celebrate their strengths! As you share the cupcakes or cookies with the students, show them the train or car. Tell students you're going to read *I Knew You Could! A Book for All the Stops in Your Life* (show train) and *What the Road Said* (show car) to celebrate their strengths and to encourage students to keep using their strengths on the journey ahead.

Definition: Review definitions of Resilient, Innovative, and Connecting.

Book Share: Read *I Knew You Could! A Book for All the Stops in Your Life* by Craig Dorfman and/or *What the Road Said* by Cleo Wade.

Discussion: Congratulate students for their amazing strengths! Then have students share one or two strengths from their Strengths Bubble Maps with the class. After each student shares, give affirmation (e.g., three big claps, round of applause, class cheer).

Reflection: Have students put a small box in the top right-hand corner of their Strengths Bubble Maps.

Extension: Choose any of the following activities to continue to celebrate strengths:

- Attach a copy of the letter on page 73 to each student's Strengths Bubble Map. Have students take their Strengths Bubble Maps home to share with their families. Students can bring their bubble maps back to class to make copies, including any strengths added by parents. Then they can bring their Strengths Bubble Maps back home to display somewhere.

- Continue to focus on strengths by creating a "brag bag" for each student. Have each student decorate a bag. Throughout the year, whenever the student receives a compliment from someone, record the "brag" on a 3 x 5 card to put in the bag. You can have 3 x 5 cards easily available for students to record their own brags as well. At the end of the school year, before sending the bags home, have students open their bags and read the brags to celebrate all they've accomplished.

SPECIAL NOTE

You will want to keep a color copy of each student's strengths bubble map for displaying/referring to in your class. A color copy will also be needed for use with lessons 19 and 20.

> Students with dyslexia have an island
> of weakness in a sea of strengths.
> —**Sally Shaywitz**

Dear Parent,

Your child has been discovering their strengths, specifically in being Resilient, Innovative, and Connecting (see definitions below). By focusing on their strengths, children can increase their self-esteem and decrease their anxiety.

During our time together, we have read books about being Resilient, Innovative, and Connecting and discovered inspirational people with dyslexia who exhibit those strengths. Your child recorded examples of their own strengths in a color-coded Strengths Bubble Map, which is attached. Please read the Strengths Bubble Map with your child and celebrate their strengths together. You can add any additional strengths to the map. Display it at home to help them remember their strengths.

Your child has brilliant strengths!

Sincerely,

Resilient: to keep going even when something is hard, even when you make mistakes, and even when you're afraid

Innovative: to create, invent, and see things in a different way; to "think outside the box"

Connecting: to show kindness, to work together, and to communicate well with others

Just Read! by Lori Degman

Materials:
> *Just Read!* by Lori Degman
> about 20–25 book selections from the lesson extension sections
> table cloth, hot chocolate, cups, spoons, marshmallows, whipped cream, sprinkles, a sign that says "Starbooks" (optional)

Introduction: Show *Just Read!* by Lori Degman. Share with students that the author, Lori Degman, struggled with reading as a child but now reads all the time. Tell students that it is exciting to read no matter the genre of book and no matter where they are. Today, they are at "Starbooks," a place to discover a good book and a good cup of hot chocolate.

Book Share: Before reading, have the students make their cup of hot chocolate. While students are drinking their hot chocolate, read *Just Read!* by Lori Degman.

Discussion: Tell students you are going to show them different kinds of books. Walk around the room to the book selections. Stop at each genre group. Show each title. When finished with each genre group, ask students to show thumb up for "yes," they are interested in one of those books, thumb down for "no," they are not interested in one of those books, or thumb in the middle if they are "unsure" and may need to look at the selections some more.

Reflection: Give each student five to six sticky notes. Have them write their names on the sticky notes. Afterwards, have students walk around the room. As they find books they are interested in, have them place their sticky note on the cover of the book. When students are finished placing their sticky notes on books they are interested in, take a photo of them holding their book choices. Share this photo with their parents so the parents also know their child's choices (this is especially helpful to do right before the holidays). Also print a copy of the photo out for the students so the students can take the photo to the school library, community library, or town bookstore or look up their selections on Learning Ally, Bookshare, Epic, or Playaway.

Extension: Choose any of the following activities:

- A school or community library can be an intimidating place for some students. Set up a time to meet with the school or community librarian to not only show the students where to locate their books of interest but also explain how the books are organized.
- Students enjoy giving book recommendations. Create a weekly sign up for students who would like to recommend a book. Give students an opportunity to read their favorite part or page of the book to the class (this becomes a safe place for those who are intimidated by reading).

Zach has a great sense of humor and connected to books by Dav Pilkey. His mom texted this photo of Zach. He is reading AND enjoying this book. This is why we do what we do.

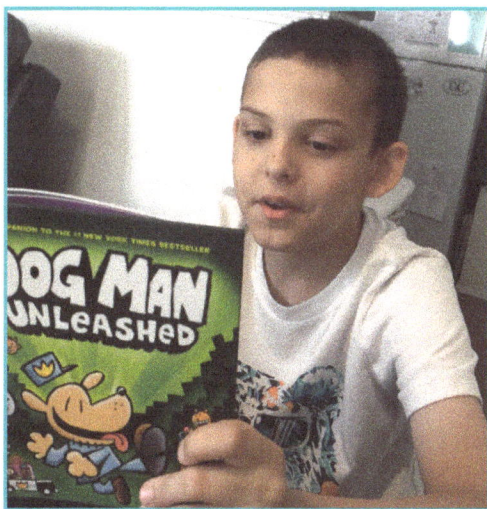

SPECIAL NOTE

This is an exciting lesson to celebrate reading and to engage students in reading! It is an amazing opportunity to connect your students with books they are interested in. Students who are very leery of books find this to be a safe environment to browse books and discover their interests.

HELPFUL HINT

If you don't have the books in your personal library, plan to check them out from your school or community library ahead of time. Set up the book selections around your room so students see all the different books when they walk in. Organize the books by genre (e.g., all the graphic novels together, all the sports books together, all the joke books together).

risk-taker

dreamer

determined

creative

brave

confident

unique

storyteller

entertainer

imaginer

maker

mover

questioner

"people" people

Part VI

EXPLORE MORE : ADDITIONAL LESSONS ON STUDENTS' STRENGTHS

> **Before beginning these lessons, have the following books on hand:**
>
> *Inspire Your Power: An Inspirational Journal of Love and Joy for Kids with Dyslexia* by Karlayna Platt
>
> *Xtraordinary People: Made by Dyslexia* by Kate Griggs

Inspire Your Power: An Inspirational Journal of Love and Joy for Kids with Dyslexia by Karlayna Platt

Materials:
> Definition Cards (Resilient, Innovative, Connecting)
> *Inspire Your Power: An Inspirational Journal of Love and Joy for Kids with Dyslexia* by Karlayna Platt
> color copies of students' Strengths Bubble Maps
> one blue marker for each student

Definition: Review definitions of Resilient, Innovative, and Connecting.

Book Share: Read *Inspire Your Power: An Inspirational Journal of Love and Joy for Kids with Dyslexia* by Karlayna Platt.

Discussion: On the board, write these words referred to in the book: risk-taker, dreamer, determined, creative, brave, unique, confident. Ask students the following questions:
• Which words are powers that describe you?
• How does Karlayna's journal encourage you?
• How does Karlayna's journal help you see your power?

Reflection: Encourage students to share one or more of the listed words they relate to. Write their listed word(s) on their Strengths Bubble Map (or have students write it on their own or using speech-to-text in a Google Doc or Seesaw text page). Have students use a blue marker to bubble outline each word.

student

Determined

Brave

Creative

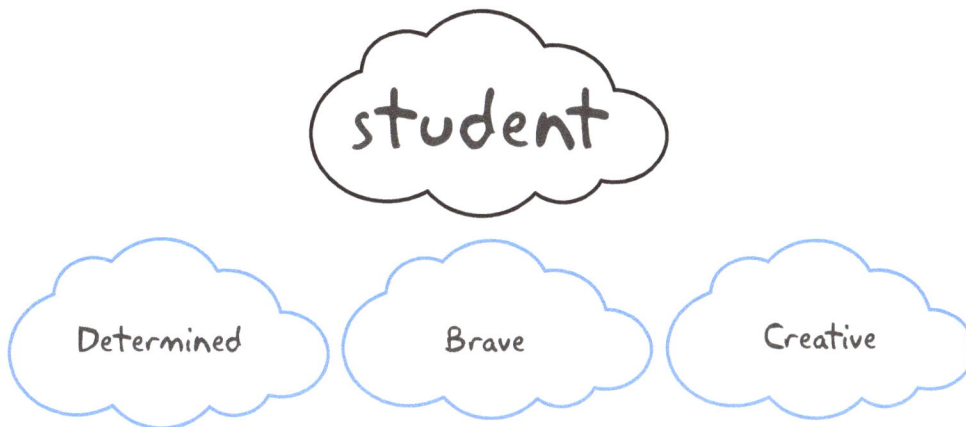

Extension: Choose any of the following activities to continue to explore more:

- Read more about Karlayna Platt and her journey with dyslexia: https://southlake.bubblelife.com/community/southlake_reporter/library/35662481/key/355474491/Local_15_yo_girl_authors_book_INSPIRE_YOUR_POWER_Inspirational_book_for_Children_with_Dyslexia
- Read about dyslexia from the point of view of twelve-year-old Jennifer Smith in *Dyslexia Wonders: Understanding the Daily Life of a Dyslexic from a Child's Point of View.*

SPECIAL NOTE

Inspire Your Power: An Inspirational Journal of Love and Joy for Kids with Dyslexia by Karlayna Platt and *Dyslexia Wonders: Understanding the Daily Life of a Dyslexic from a Child's Point of View* are both from the student's perspective—a valuable one to share.

Xtraordinary People by Kate Griggs

Materials:
> a photo of each student
> Definition Cards (Resilient, Innovative, Connecting)
> *Xtraordinary People: Made by Dyslexia* by Kate Griggs
> one device connected to the internet for each student to take the Xtraordinary People Quiz
> color copies of students' Strengths Bubble Maps
> one blue marker for each student

Introduction: Place photos of your students in a bag. Have a student pull the photos out of the bag. Tell students they are "Xtraordinary" and that you're going to read a book about finding out how each student is Xtraordinary.

Definition: Review definitions of Resilient, Innovative, and Connecting.

Book Share: Read *Xtraordinary People: Made by Dyslexia* by Kate Griggs or listen to HRH Princess Beatrice read the book: https://www.youtube.com/watch?v=h6f8QVnDXfU (13:04).

Discussion: On the board, write these "people" words referred to in the book: storyteller, entertainer, imaginer, maker, mover, questioner, "people" people. Hand out devices for students to take the Xtraordinary People Quiz on the following website: https://www.madebydyslexia.org/kids-quiz/.

Read the choices aloud for each section, and have students click in the boxes next to the choices that relate to them. When students are finished, have them click "submit." It will then share the results of their quiz. Students can read their results or use Speechify to have their results read to them, or you can print out the results and read them aloud to the students.

Reflection: Encourage students to share their Xtraordinary type(s). Write their Xrtraordinary type(s) on their Strengths Bubble Map (or have students write it on their own or using speech-to-text in a Google Doc or Seesaw text page). Have students use a black marker to bubble outline each word.

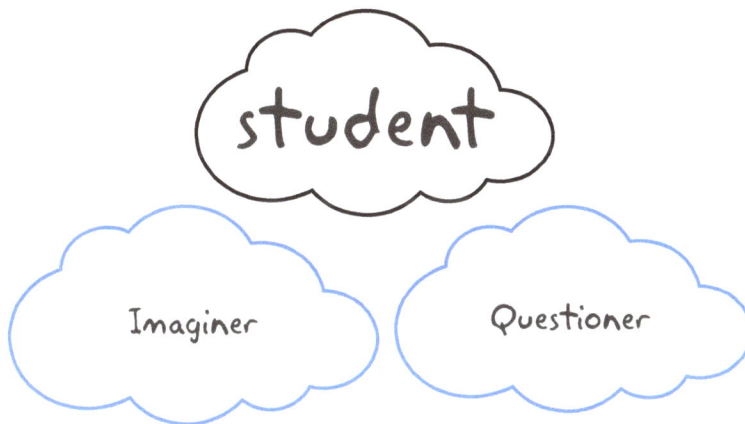

student

Imaginer

Questioner

Extension: Read about more Xtraordinary people in *The Bigger Picture Book of Amazing Dyslexics and the Jobs They Do* by Kathy Iwanczak Forsyth and Kate Power.

Part VII

PARENTS AND TEACHERS, DISCOVER YOUR STRENGTHS

> **Before beginning these lessons,
> have the following books on hand:**
> *Now, Discover Your Strengths*
> by Marcus Buckingham and Donald Clifton
> *What's Your Shine?* by Claudia Beeny

Now, Discover Your Strengths by Marcus Buckingham and Donald Clifton and ***What's Your Shine?*** by Dr. Claudia Beeny

Teachers and parents interested in discovering your own strengths, this is for you!

Materials:

> *Now, Discover Your Strengths* by Marcus Buckingham and Donald Clifton
> *What's Your Shine?* by Dr. Claudia Beeny

Book Summaries:

Now, Discover Your Strengths by Marcus Buckingham and Donald Clifton

Encouraging you to focus more on your strengths than your weaknesses, this book defines the thirty-four talents and provides the code for the CliftonStrengths assessment. To complete your talent assessment and discover your top five strengths, you can use your access code from inside the book, or you can purchase an access code at https://store.gallup.com/p/en-us/10108/top-5-cliftonstrengths.

Reflection: After taking the assessment, record your top five strengths. Read about the strengths in the resource provided in the book or online. Once you discover your top strengths, think about how you'll use them not only for your own self-improvement but also to help others.

What's Your Shine? by Dr. Claudia Beeny

In *What's Your Shine?*, Dr. Beeny encourages you to discover your unique combination of **S**trengths, **H**obbies, **I**nterests/Irritants, **N**eeds, and **E**xperiences, your "SHINE." Not only will you discover your shine, but you'll also learn to apply those gifts to make the world a better place. (https://www.houseofshine.com/)

Reflection: As you discover your shine, record your strengths, hobbies, interests/irritants, needs, and experiences, then record your talent, interest, and need to discover your "point of intersection."

SPECIAL NOTE

If you have yet to take inventory of your own strengths, these books provide the ideal opportunity for you to begin.

Part VIII

APPENDIX

EXTENSION BOOKS

(in order introduced in lessons)

RESILIENT

Y Is for Yet: A Growth Mindset Alphabet by Shannon Anderson

Where the Red Fern Grows by Wilson Rawls

Mistakes that Worked: The World's Familiar Inventions and How They Came to Be
    by Charlotte Foltz Jones

Telescopes for Kids: A Junior Scientist's Guide to Stargazing, Constellations,
    and Discovering Far-Off Galaxies by Vanessa Thomas

Who Was? series by various authors

Spectacular Stories for Curious Kids by Jesse Sullivan

Fish in a Tree by Lynda Mullaly Hunt

Wilma Jean the Worry Machine by Julia Cook

Courage by Bernard Waber

What to Do When You Worry Too Much: A Kid's Guide to Overcoming Anxiety
    by Dawn Huebner

INNOVATIVE

Kid Innovators: True Tales of Childhood from Inventors and Trailblazers
    by Robin Stevenson

The Floor Is Lava: And 99 More Games for Everyone, Everywhere by Ivan Brett

The Way I Feel by Janan Cain

My Many Colored Days by Dr. Seuss

ABC Book of Feelings by Marlys Boddy

In My Heart: A Book of Feelings by Jo Witek

Don't Pop Your Cork on Mondays! The Children's Anti-Stress Book by Adolph Moser

Don't Feed the Monster on Tuesdays! The Children's Self-Esteem Book
    by Adolph Moser

Don't Rant and Rave on Wednesdays! The Children's Anger-Control Book by Adolph Moser

Don't Despair on Thursdays! The Children's Grief-Management Book by Adolph Moser

Tartine All Day: Modern Recipes for the Home Cook by Elisabeth Prueitt

Bake Up! Kids Cookbook: Go from Beginner to Pro with 60 Recipes and Essential Techniques by Nicole Hendizadeh

Spy School series by Stuart Gibbs

Swindle series by Gordon Korman

Ballpark Mysteries series by David A. Kelly

If You're Reading This, It's Too Late by Pseudonymous Bosch

Escape From Mr. Lemoncello's Library by Chris Grabenstein

The Body Under the Piano by Marthe Jocelyn

Charlie & Frog: A Mystery by Karen Kane

Digging for Trouble by Lina Fairstein

Clubhouse Mysteries: Lost in the Tunnel of Time by Sharon M. Draper

Me, Frida, and the Secret of the Peacock Ring by Angela Cervantes

Case Closed #1: Mystery in the Mansion by Lauren Magaziner

And Then There Were None and other mysteries by Agatha Christie

Ish by Peter Reynolds

Linnea in Monet's Garden by Christina Bjork

Grandpa and the Library: How Charles White Learned to Paint by C. Ian White

Frida Kahlo and Her Animalitos by Monica Brown

Captain Underpants series by Dav Pilkey

Dog Man series by Dav Pilkey

Elephant & Piggie series by Mo Willems

The Pigeon series by Mo Willems

Narwhal and Jelly series by Ben Clanton

Big Nate series by Lincoln Peirce

Phoebe and Her Unicorn series by Dana Simpson

Diary of a Wimpy Kid series by Jeff Kinney

Sunny Side Up series by Jennifer L. Holm

New Kid by Jerry Craft

CONNECTING

Wonder by R. J. Palacio

The Royal Bee by Frances and Ginger Park

The Elephant's New Shoe by Laurel Neme

The Invisible Boy by Trudy Ludwig

The Kindness Book by Todd Parr

Amazing Athletes series by various authors

Ballpark Mysteries series by David A. Kelly

Victory School Superstars series by various authors

Playing with Purpose series by Mike Yorkey

Comeback Kids series by Mike Lupica

Home Team series by Mike Lupica

Who Was? series by various authors

Middle School Rules series by Sean Jensen

The Contract series by Derek Jeter and Paul Mantrell

Knock Knock Jokes for Funny Kids by Jimmy Jones

Laugh-Out-Loud: The 1,001 Funniest LOL Jokes of All Time by Rob Elliott

Acts of Kindness by Melissa Cenatiempo

Will You Be the "I" in Kind? by Julia Cook

EXPLORE MORE

Dyslexia Wonders: Understanding the Daily Life of a Dyslexic from a Child's Point of View by Jennifer Smith

The Bigger Picture Book of Amazing Dyslexics and the Jobs They Do by Kathy Iwanczak Forsyth and Kate Power

EXTENSION RESOURCES
(in order introduced in lessons)

RESILIENT
Interview with Steven Spielberg by Quinn Bradlee, a student with dyslexia:

    https://www.youtube.com/watch?v=-lGr840jE_0 (10:55)

Interview with actress Keira Knightly:

    https://www.youtube.com/watch?v=OLb6ehPPc4E (4:03)

Speechify app

Interview with Richard Branson:

    https://www.youtube.com/watch?v=-OZyXZ__5TU (4:33)

Interview with Charles Schwab:

    https://www.youtube.com/watch?v=ZLHQPRCCkcs (10:02)

Biography about Nelson Rockefeller, former vice president with dyslexia:

    http://dyslexiahelp.umich.edu/success-stories/nelson-rockefeller

SkyView app

Movie: *Luca* (1:35:00)

Movie: *Leap* (1:29:00)

Video of Darcey Bussell dancing a solo:

    https://www.youtube.com/watch?v=We7KAkWJow8 (2:11)

Interview with Darcey Bussell:

    https://www.youtube.com/watch?v=_6tRLwR2QEs (3:25)

INNOVATIVE
Apps: AMAZE!, codeSpark Academy (ages 4–9), ScratchJr (ages 5–7), Scratch (ages 8–16), Mimo app (ages 12 and up)

Interview with Maria Naggaga about interactive learning and coding:

    https://docs.microsoft.com/en-us/shows/On-NET/Maria-Naggaga-Interactive-learning-with-Try-NET (12:56)

Article about Jack Horner, paleontologist and professor with dyslexia:

    http://dyslexiahelp.umich.edu/success-stories/jack-horner

Game Cat Crimes:

*https://www.amazon.com/ThinkFun-Crimes-Logic-Brainteaser-Girls/dp/
B07616B2NS?th=1*

Video of Eric Carle creating his "picture writings":

https://www.youtube.com/watch?v=S0lNNN6jh74 (32:07)

Interview with Dav Pilkey by kid reporter William Russell:

https://www.youtube.com/watch?v=be1l4y-eflY (1:15)

How to create graphics like Dav Pilkey:

https://www.youtube.com/watch?v=Y5MgYqkvuwM (3:09)

"How To Help Reluctant Readers Love Books: Advice from Dav Pilkey":

https://www.scholastic.com/parents/family-life/parent-child/qa-captain-underpants-
author-dav-pilkey.html

Free printable comic book templates:

https://picklebums.com/free-printable-comic-book-templates/

CONNECTING

Movie: *Dolphin Tale* (1:54:00)

Interview with Patricia Palocco about how the original Mr. Falker changed her life:

https://www.youtube.com/watch?v=4uxlMV8uJAs (1:58)

Biographies of athletes with dyslexia:

Olympian rower Steve Redgrave: http://dyslexiahelp.umich.edu/steve-redgrave

Major League Baseball player Nolan Ryan:

http://dyslexiahelp.umich.edu/success-stories/nolan-ryan

NFL football player Tim Tebow:

http://dyslexiahelp.umich.edu/success-stories/tim-tebow

Interview with comedian Jay Leno:

https://www.youtube.com/watch?v=gkFPsFVo7zw (0:58)

Interview with comedian Whoopi Goldberg:

https://www.youtube.com/watch?v=IMBDPOXbAHo (5:12)

Interview with HRH Princess Beatrice:

https://www.youtube.com/watch?v=JrSV-rLaVCA (3:39)

"50 Acts of Kindness for Kids to Do to Make the World a Better Place":

https://www.rd.com/article/acts-of-kindness-for-kids/

Article about painted rock trail:

https://www.dallasnews.com/arts-entertainment/lifestyle/2020/10/16/new-tourist-attraction-in-grapevine-started-as-act-of-kindness-during-covid-19-pandemic/

EXPLORE MORE

Karlayna Platt's story about her journey with dyslexia:

https://southlake.bubblelife.com/community/southlake_reporter/library/35662481/key/355474491/Local_15_yo_girl_authors_book_INSPIRE_YOUR_POWER_Inspirational_book_for_Children_with_Dyslexia

PARENTS AND TEACHERS, DISCOVER YOUR STRENGTHS

Top 5 Clifton Strengths: https://store.gallup.com/p/en-us/10108/top-5-cliftonstrengths

House of Shine's website: https://www.houseofshine.com/

RECOMMENDED RESOURCES

DYSLEXIA

Books for Students Recently Diagnosed with Dyslexia

Use these books to explain what dyslexia is, how the dyslexic brain works, and how people with dyslexia relate emotionally.

Brilliantly Dyslexic by Liz Trudeau

I Have Dyslexia by David Hurford, PhD (It is offered with either a boy or a girl on the cover.)

It's Called Dyslexia by Jennifer Moore-Mallinos

Tom's Special Talent by Kate Gaynor

The Illustrated Guide to Dyslexia and Its Amazing People by Kate Power and Kathy Iwanczak Forsyth

Books for Adults to Learn More about Dyslexia

Your state's dyslexia handbook. For example, *The Dyslexia Handbook* from Texas: https://tea.texas.gov/sites/default/files/2018-Dyslexia-Handbook_Approved_Accomodated_12_11_2018.pdf

Overcoming Dyslexia by Sally Shaywitz

About Dyslexia: Unraveling the Myth by Priscilla Vail

Basic Facts about Dyslexia & Other Reading Problems by Louisa Cook Moats and Karen Dakin

The Dyslexia Empowerment Plan: A Blueprint for Renewing Your Child's Confidence and Love of Learning by Ben Foss

Dyslexia Wonders: Understanding the Daily Life of a Dyslexic from a Child's Point of View by Jennifer Smith

Teaching a Struggling Reader: One Mom's Experience with Dyslexia: A Guide for Parents and Teachers Who Want to Start Learning about Dyslexia (DOG ON A LOG Parent and Teacher Guides Book 1) by Pamela Brookes

The Secret Life of the Dyslexic Child by Robert Frank, PhD

Websites for Adults to Learn More about Dyslexia

International Dyslexia Association: https://www.dyslexiaida.org

This complete site provides needed and valuable information and resources about dyslexia. The About Dyslexia, Families, and Resources tabs are especially useful, providing information like the definition of dyslexia, a self-assessment test, and frequently asked questions. Most helpful are the Fact Sheets, which can be found under either the About Dyslexia or Families tabs. The Fact Sheets cover the basic facets of dyslexia and the components that interrelate such as "AD/HD and Dyslexia," "Gifted and Dyslexic," "Spelling," "Assessment of Dyslexia," and "Transitioning from High School to College."

The Scottish Rite Hospital/Luke Waites Center for Dyslexia: http://www.tsrhc.org/dyslexia

This valuable site provides basic information about dyslexia, the eligibility to be provided free dyslexia therapy services (if you live in the Northeast Texas area), the curriculum taught in the program, dyslexia laws, and links for educational seminars for parents and teachers.

The Yale Center for Dyslexia & Creativity: https://www.dyslexia.yale.edu

The Yale Center for Dyslexia & Creativity is a major contributor to brain research for dyslexia. This website includes not only the scientific information that describes the dyslexic brain but also useful tabs for parents and educators. For parents, there are resources that aid in identifying dyslexia at each developmental stage, related reading skills, and tools to help their children at home. For educators, stories of dyslexic students are provided, along with reading lists and technology aides. There is also a valuable tab with lists of successful dyslexics in the areas of the arts, science, business, education, medicine, and public service.

Made by Dyslexia: https://www.madebydyslexia.org/

Designed to redefine dyslexia by helping the world understand, value, and support dyslexia, this website not only provides essential resources for parents, teachers, and students but also provides helpful educator and workplace guides.

Understood: https://www.understood.org/articles/en/what-is-dyslexia

This website contains resources for parents and caregivers who care about their child's learning and thinking differences and who want to help their child's behaviors, learning, and everyday skills. Topics include dyslexia, ADHD, dyscalculia, and written expression disorder.

Dyslexia Help: http://dyslexiahelp.umich.edu/

Overflowing with practical and helpful resources for parents, teachers, and professionals, this website provides tools from dyslexia assessment quizzes and reading programs to success stories and fun apps and games.

Multisensory Teaching Approach: https://www.ortonacademy.org/resources/what-is-the-orton-gillingham-approach/

On this site, you will find vital information explaining the multisensory teaching approach used in dyslexia curriculum. Information from founding researchers of this approach, Dr. Orton and Anna Gillingham, is located under the home/approach tab.

Lexicon Reading Center: http://www.lexiconreadingcenter.org

This site provides information not only on dyslexia but also on dysgraphia and dyscalculia, disabilities that can often occur with dyslexia. A variety of links and resources are provided for both parents and educators that describe symptoms, programs, technology aides, and workshops.

Experience Dyslexia® Kit: https://norcal.dyslexiaida.org/experience-dyslexia/experience-dyslexia-kit

This website provides information to purchase a kit or attend a workshop that simulates what it is like to have dyslexia.

Videos about Dyslexia

Dyslexia: A Hidden Disability

https://www.youtube.com/watch?v=8m1fCz3ohMw (6:45)

Narrated by Sally Shaywitz, this video explains what dyslexia is and provides tidbits from people of different ages and occupations who have dyslexia: Charles Swab, Whoopi Goldberg, lawyers, surgeons, college students, and elementary students.

The Big Picture: Rethinking Dyslexia https://www.amazon.com/Big-Picture-Richard-Branson/dp/B00FPZXUGQ (52:00)

The full docudrama version of the above video clip.

From Dyslexic Struggling Reader to Valedictorian https://www.youtube.com/watch?v=1_8o_FHsfnk (3:02)

In this video, Dustin Henderson shares about his journey with dyslexia and how he uses his strengths.

Learning Differently: Our Thoughts on Dyslexia https://www.youtube.com/watch?v=L_rdls_YIXU (4:53)

This video explores dyslexia from the point of view of Alison and Dylan, a seventh and fifth grader, and the tools that they use.

Sources about Text-to-Speech and Audiobooks

Learning Ally: https://learningally.org/

Providing an online library of 80,000 accessible audio textbooks, Learning Ally offers personalized support for families and helpful tools for teachers.

"I'm Not Alone in this World": William's Dyslexia Story https://www.youtube.com/watch?v=FJrHQH5Chvc (1:30)

Ten-year-old William shares about his journey with dyslexia and how reading books on Learning Ally has helped him be more independent and relate to his classmates better.

Bookshare: https://www.bookshare.org/cms/

Bookshare provides access to the largest online library of books, textbooks, newspapers, and magazines.

Epic: https://www.getepic.com/

This site provides a digital library with e-books and audiobooks for kids twelve and under.

Your Local Library

Visit your local library to find books on CD, audiobooks, and Playaway books.

Speechify: https://speechify.com/

Having dyslexia, Cliff Weitzman developed this app that can be used to have text read aloud using a computer generated voice.

Text to Speech on an iPad (or any iOS device) https://www.youtube.com/watch?v=rSP0UFoyBYo (0:36)

A quick instructional video about how to use text-to-speech on an iPad.

Sources about Speech-to-Text

Voice to Text: Go Dyslexia Vlog on Voicetyping for Google Docs https://www.youtube.com/watch?v=INZwzqKZR1E&t=8s (5:57)

A tutorial from Dr. Erika Warren on how to use speech-to-text in a Google Doc.

Dictation on a Mac https://www.youtube.com/watch?v=77tm3sgwRP0 (2:08)

A tutorial from Tech Talk America on how to use the dictation tool on a Mac.

How to use Seesaw (Text Tool and Microphone): https://app.seesaw.me/activities/ri94d3/how-to-use-seesaw-text-tool-and-microphone

Used in many schools, Seesaw provides this tutorial for using speech-to-text.

Books and Websites for Adults to Learn about Laws and Rights

Any of the following books written by Peter and Pamela Wright:

Wrightslaw: Special Education Law

Wrightslaw: All about IEPs

Wrightslaw: From Emotions to Advocacy

Wrightslaw: All about Tests and Assessments.

Wrightslaw: http://www.wrightslaw.com

This website provides an extensive list of special education topics, the laws that correlate, all the rights of parents, and useful information for school meetings such as an Individual Education Plan (IEP). Numerous helpful links are provided for parents and educators.

The Legal Framework: https://framework.esc18.net/display/Webforms/ LandingPage.aspx

For parents in Texas interested in the specific laws that correlate with dyslexia, you can input your district number (e.g., 220906), select a disability, and find the corresponding service and law.

Advocacy and Support

Stand Up LD: https://www.standupld.org

This organization supports parents of children with learning differences and informs educators about children with learning differences. This group provides resources and meetings to help parents and children with learning differences advocate for themselves.

Reversed: A Memoir by Lois Letchford

READ: Reaching Educating and Advocating for Dyslexia: https://www.navigatelifetexas.org/en/services-groups-events/parent-groups/ read-reaching-educating-and-advocating-for-dyslexia

Founded by parents, this advocacy website provides valuable information and helpful resources for those who live in the Grapevine/Colleyville, Texas area. This area group also provides a mentorship program between older students with dyslexia and younger students with dyslexia. If you're not in the northeast Texas area, find a support group where you live.

THE BRAIN AND EXECUTIVE FUNCTION

Books for Students to Learn about the Brain

Your Fantastic Elastic Brain: Stretch It, Shape It by JoAnn Deak, PhD

A Walk in the Rain with A Brain by Edward Hallowell

Books for Adults to Learn More about the Brain and Learning

Emotions: The On/Off Switch for Learning by Priscilla Vail

How the Brain Learns by David A. Sousa

Overcoming Dyslexia by Sally Shaywitz

Books for Students to Learn about Executive Function

The following books, written by Julia Cook (https://www.juliacookonline.com/), are ideal for helping students understand executive function:

Planning Isn't My Priority… and Making Priorities Isn't in My Plans!

Study Skilled…NOT!

The PROcrastinator

I Can't Find My Whatchamacallit!!

Be Where Your Feet Are!

My Mouth is a Volcano

Books and Websites for Adults to Learn More about Executive Function

The following books by Peg Dawson and Richard Guare (https://www.smartbutscatteredkids.com/) provide explanations and tools for executive function:

Smart but Scattered

Smart but Scattered Teens

Smart but Scattered—and Stalled

Executive Skills in Children and Adolescents

The Smart but Scattered Guide to Success

Coaching Students with Executive Skills Deficits

Executive Function 101 (e-book):
https://www.chconline.org/resourcelibrary/
executive-function-101-e-book-downloadable/
This free PDF authored by the National Center for Learning Disabilities explains the basics of executive function (planning, organizing, paying attention) and discusses the three areas most affected: learning, behavior and emotions, and social situations and relationships.

Understood: https://www.understood.org/articles/en/what-is-executive-function
This website contains resources for parents and caregivers who care about their child's learning and thinking differences and who want to help their child's behaviors, learning, and everyday skills. Topics include executive function, ADHD, social skills challenges, and sensory processing challenges.

EFs 2 the Rescue: http://efs2therescue.com/
This site lists ten animated characters who demonstrate areas of executive function:
Aware Bear: Metacognition
Emotibot: Emotional Control
Flexi Lexi: Flexibility
Get Up & Go: Task Initiation
Gracie Goal Getter: Goal-Directed Persistence
Plan Man: Planning and Organization
ReME: Working Memory
Stop-a-Tron: Response Inhibition
Susie Shifter: Shifting and Time Management
Sustain-O, the Great: Sustained Attention

Curriculum and Websites for Adults to Learn More about Emotional Regulation
The Zones of Regulation™ by Leah Kuypers:
https://www.socialthinking.com/zones-of-regulation

Superflex Takes on Glassman and the Team of Unthinkables™
by Michelle Garcia Winner:
https://www.socialthinking.com/Products/
superflex-takes-on-glassman-team-of-unthinkables

ADHD

Books for Students Who Have ADHD

I Have Ants in My Pants, *It's Hard to Be a Verb*, and *Personal Space Camp*
by Julia Cook

Marvin's Monster Diary: ADHD Attacks! (But I Rock It, Big Time) by Raun Melmed

Learning to Slow Down and Pay Attention: A Book for Kids about ADHD
by Kathleen Nadeau

Cory Stories: A Kid's Book about Living with ADHD by Jeanne Kraus

*Thriving with ADHD Workbook for Kids: 60 Fun Activities to Help Children
Self-Regulate, Focus, and Succeed* by Kelli Miller

A Dragon with ADHD: A Children's Story about ADHD by Steve Herman

Books for Adults to Learn More about ADHD

All Dogs Have ADHD by Kathy Hoopmann (A photo book that explains ADHD
in a simple format—can also be read to students.)

*Driven to Distraction: Recognizing and Coping with Attention Deficit Disorder from
Childhood through Adulthood* by Edward M. Hallowell MD and John J. Ratey MD

*From ABC to ADHD: What Every Parent Should Know about Dyslexia and
Attention Problems* by Eric Tridas

REFERENCES

Ahlberg, A. (2018). *The pencil* (B. Ingman, Illus.). Walker.

Andersen, C. H. (2021, October 13). *50 Acts of kindness for kids to do to make the world a better place.* Reader's Digest. https://www.rd.com/article/acts-of-kindness-for-kids/

Anderson, S., & Souva, J. (2020). *Y is for yet: A growth mindset alphabet.* Free Spirit Publishing.

Barbalich, A. (n.d.). *How to help reluctant readers love books: Advice from Dav Pilkey.* Scholastic. https://www.scholastic.com/parents/family-life/parent-child/qa-captain-underpants-author-dav-pilkey.html

Beaty, A. (2013). *Rosie Revere, engineer* (D. Roberts, Illus.). Abrams Books for Young Readers.

Beaty, A. (2019). *Sofia Valdez, future prez* (D. Roberts, Illus.). Abrams Books for Young Readers.

Beeny, C. (2020). *What's your shine?* CKB Group.

Beeny, C. (2021, September 5). *Home.* House of Shine. https://www.houseofshine.com/

Berger, S. (2018). *What if…* (M. Curato, Illus.). Little, Brown and Company.

Bjork, C. (2012). *Linnea in Monet's garden* (L. Anderson, Illus.). Sourcebooks Jabberwocky.

Boddy, M. (1991). *Abc book of feelings* (J. Boddy, Illus.). Concordia.

Bosch. P. (2008). *If you're reading this, it's too late.* Little, Brown Books for Young Readers.

Brett, I. (2019). *The floor is lava: And 99 more games for everyone, everywhere.* Headline Home.

Brown, M. (2019). *Frida Kahlo and her animalitos* (J. Parra, Illus.). North-South Books.

Cain, J. (2001). *The way I feel.* Scholastic.

Cenatiempo, M. (2021). Acts of kindness (P. Ablal, Illus.).

Cervantes, A. (2019). *Me, Frida, and the secret of the peacock ring.* Scholastic.

Child Mind Institute. (2017, May 31). *Dyslexia and what I would tell #myyoungerself: Jay Leno* [Video]. YouTube. https://www.youtube.com/watch?v=gkFPsFVo7zw

Christie, A. (2020). *And then there were none*. Collins.

Clanton, B. (2016). *Narwhal and Jelly*. Tundra Books.

Clifton, D. O., & Buckingham, M. (2001). *Now, discover your strengths*. The Free Press.

Cook, J. (2021). *Bubble gum brain: Ready, get mindset...grow!* (A. Valentine, Illus.). National Center for Youth Issues.

Cook, J. (2021). *Will you be the "I" in kind?* (J. Tejido, Illus.). National Center for Youth Issues.

Cook, J. (2021). *Wilma Jean the worry machine* (A. DuFalla, Illus.). National Center for Youth Issues.

Craft, J. (2019). *New kid*. Harper.

Degman, L. (2019). *Just read!* (V. Tentler-Krylov, Illus.). Sterling Children's Books.

DiOrio, R. (2020). *What does it mean to be kind?* (S. Jorisch, Illus.). Encantos.

Dorfman, C. (2018). *I knew you could! A book for all the stops in your life* (C. Ong, Illus.). Platt & Munk.

Draper, S. M. (2006). *Clubhouse mysteries: Lost in the tunnel of time* (J. J. Watson, Illus.). Aladdin Paperbacks.

EFs 2 the Rescue. (n.d.). *Emotibot: Emotional control*. http://efs2therescue.com/emotibot-emotional-control/

Elliot, R. (2022). *Laugh-out-loud: The 1,001 funniest lol jokes of all time*. HarperCollins.

Elliott, R. (2013). *Knock-knock jokes for kids*. Revell.

Fairstein, L. (2017). Digging for trouble. Dial Books.

FriendsOfQuinn. (2014, September 9). *Founder Quinn Bradlee talks dyslexia with Whoopi Goldberg* [Video]. YouTube. https://www.youtube.com/watch?v=IMBDPOXbAHo

Gibbs, S. (2012). *Spy school*. Simon & Schuster Books for Young Readers.

Grabenstein, C. (2014). *Escape from Mr. Lemoncello's library*. Yearling.

GrahamBensinger. (2019, October 9). *Charles Schwab on dyslexia: I struggle with the alphabet* [Video]. YouTube. https://www.youtube.com/watch?v=ZLHQPRCCkcs

Granados, M. G. (2020, October 16). *Parr Park Rock Trail in Grapevine started as act of kindness during COVID-19 pandemic*. The Dallas Morning News. https://www.dallasnews.com/arts-entertainment/lifestyle/2020/10/16/new-tourist-at-traction-in-grapevine-started-as-act-of-kindness-during-covid-19-pandemic/

Griggs, K. (2021). *Xtraordinary people: Made by dyslexia*. Penguin Random House Children's.

Hendizadeh, N. (2020). *Bake up! Kids cookbook: Go from beginner to pro with 60 recipes and essential techniques*. Zeitgeist.

Holm, J. L. (2015). *Sunny side up* (M. Holm, Illus.). Graphix.

Huebner, D. (2006). *What to do when you worry too much: A kid's guide to overcoming anxiety* (B. Matthews, Illus.). Magination Press.

Hunt, L. M. (2015). *Fish in a tree*. Puffin Books.

Jensen, S. *Middle school rules*. Broadstreet Publishing Group.

Jeter, D., & Mantell, P. (2016). *The contract*. Jeter Publishing.

Jocelyn, M. (2021). *The body under the piano* (I. Follath, Illus.). Tundra Books.

Jones, C. F. (2016). *Mistakes that worked: The world's familiar inventions and how they came to be* (J. O'Brien, Illus.). Delacorte Press.

Jones, J. (2018). *Knock knock jokes for funny kids*. PUBLISHER.

Kane, K. (2019). *Charlie & Frog: A mystery*. Disney-Hyperion.

Keller iReporter. (n.d.). *Local 15 y/o girl authors book: Inspire your power (inspirational book for children with dyslexia)*. Southlake BubbleLife. https://southlake.bubblelife.com/community/southlake_reporter/library/35662481/ key/355474491/Local_15_yo_girl_authors_book_INSPIRE_YOUR_POWER_ Inspirational_book_for_Children_with_Dyslexia

Kelly, D. A. *Ballpark mysteries*. Random House Books for Young Readers.

Kinney, J. (2014). *Diary of a wimpy kid*. Puffin.

Korman, G. (2015). *Swindle*. Scholastic Press.

Kuypers, L. M. (2011). *The zones of regulation: A curriculum designed to foster self-regulation and emotional control*. Social Thinking.

Lander, R. (2018, February 19). *Maria Naggaga: Interactive Learning with try.NET*. Microsoft Docs. https://docs.microsoft.com/en-us/shows/On-NET/ Maria-Naggaga-Interactive-learning-with-Try-NET

LearnConfidently. (2012, October 23). *Steven Spielberg: Dyslexia interview* [Video]. YouTube. https://www.youtube.com/watch?v=-IGr840jE_0

Letchford, Lois. (2018). *Reversed: A memoir*. Acorn Publishing.

Llewellyn, C. (2009). *Why should I listen?* (M. Gordon, Illus.). Scholastic.

Ludwig, T. (2013). *Invisible boy* (P. Barton, Illus.). Random House.

Lupica, M. *Comeback kids.* Penguin Random House.

Lupica, M. *Home team.* Simon & Schuster.

Luyken, C. (2017). *The book of mistakes.* Dial Books.

Made By Dyslexia. (2017, August 2). *Richard Branson talks to made by dyslexia* [Video]. YouTube. https://www.youtube.com/watch?v=-OZyXZ__5TU

Made By Dyslexia. (2018, December 1). *Dame Darcey Bussell DBE - Madebydyslexia interview* [Video]. YouTube. https://www.youtube.com/watch?v=_6tRLwR2QEs

Made By Dyslexia. (2018, July 1). *Keira Knightley OBE: made by dyslexia interview* [Video]. YouTube. https://www.youtube.com/watch?v=OLb6ehPPc4E

Made By Dyslexia. (2020, May 23). *HRH princess Beatrice made by dyslexia interview* [Video]. YouTube. https://www.youtube.com/watch?v=JrSV-rLaVCA

Madrigal, S., Winner, M. G. (2009). *Superflex takes on Glassman and the team of unthinkables.* Think Social Pub.

Magaziner, L. (2018). *Case closed #1: Mystery in the mansion.* Katherine Tegen Books.

Moser, A. (1988). *Don't pop your cork on Mondays! The children's anti-stress book* (D. Melton, Illus.). Landmark Editions.

Moser, A. (1991). *Don't feed the monster on Tuesdays! The children's self-esteem book* (D. Melton, Illus.). Landmark Editions.

Moser, A. (1994). *Don't rant and rave on Wednesdays! The children's anger-control book* (D. Melton, Illus.). Landmark Editions.

Moser, A. (1996). *Don't despair on Thursdays! The children's grief-management book* (D. Melton, Illus.). Landmark Editions.

Neme, L. (2020). *The elephant's new shoe* (A. Landy, Illus.). Orchard Books.

Nicolson, R. (2015). *Positive dyslexia.* Rodin Books.

Oldland, N. (2017). *Up the creek.* Kids Can Press.

Palacio, R. J. (2019). *Wonder.* Penguin Books.

Park, F., & Park, G. (2013). *The royal bee* (C. Z.-Y. Zhang, Illus.). Zaner-Bloser.

Parr, T. (2019). *The don't worry book.* Little, Brown and Company.

Parr, T. (2019). *The kindness book.* Little, Brown and Company.

Parr, T. (2020). *It's okay to make mistakes.* Little, Brown and Company.

Peirce, L. (2020). *Big Nate.* Andrews McMeel Publishing.

Picklebums. (2015, June 23). *Free printable comic book templates!*
https://picklebums.com/free-printable-comic-book-templates/

Pilkey, D. (2014). *Captain underpants*. Panini.

Pilkey, D. (2016). *Dog man*. Scholastic.

Platt, K. (2021). *Inspire your power: An inspirational journal of love and joy for kids with dyslexia.*

Polacco, P. (1998). *Thank you, Mr. Falker*. Philomel Books.

Power, K., & Iwanczak Forsyth, K. (2020). *The bigger picture book of amazing dyslexics and the jobs they do*. Jessica Kingsley.

Prueitt, E. M. (2017). *Tartine all day: Modern recipes for the home cook.*
Lorena Jones Books.

Rawls, W. (2018). *Where the red fern grows*. Delacorte Press.

Reading Rockets. (2009, July 24). *The teacher who changed everything* [Video].
YouTube. https://www.youtube.com/watch?v=4uxlMV8uJAs

Reading Rockets. (2017, October 2). *Struggles with dyslexia* [Video]. YouTube.
https://www.youtube.com/watch?v=be1l4y-eflY

Reynolds, P. H. (2019). *Ish*. Library Ideas.

RoyalOperaHouse. (2018, November 21). *Sylvia: Act III solo (Darcey Bussell, the Royal Ballet)* [Video]. YouTube. https://www.youtube.com/watch?v=We7KAkWJow8

Saltzberg, B. (2010). *Beautiful oops!* Workman Publishing.

Seuss, Dr., & Fancher, L. (1996). *My many colored days*. Knopf.

Shaywitz, S. (2003). *Overcoming dyslexia*. Vintage.

Simpson, D. (2020). *Phoebe and her unicorn*. Andrews McMeel Publishing.

Smith, J. (2010). *Dyslexia wonders: Understanding the daily life of a dyslexic from a child's point of view*. Morgan James Publishing.

Spires, A. (2017). *The most magnificent thing*. Kids Can Press.

Stevenson, R. (2021). *Kid innovators: True tales of childhood from inventors and trailblazers* (A. Steinfeld, Illus.). Quirk Books.

StoryToys. (2021, May 27). *Eric Carle discusses his life and work* [Video].
YouTube. https://www.youtube.com/watch?v=S0INNN6jh74

Sullivan, J. (2021). *Spectacular stories for curious kids* (D. Ratkovic, Illus.). Big Dreams Kids Books.

TheScholasticChannel. (2019, December 10). *Dav Pilkey: teach graphix week* [Video]. YouTube. https://www.youtube.com/watch?v=Y5MgYqkvuwM

Thomas, V. (2021). *Telescopes for kids: A junior scientist's guide to stargazing, constellations, and discovering far-off galaxies.* Rockridge Press.

Trudeau, L. (2021). *Brilliantly dyslexic.*

University of Michigan. (n.d.). *Jack Horner.* Dyslexia Help. http://dyslexiahelp.umich.edu/success-stories/jack-horner

University of Michigan. (n.d.). *Nelson Rockefeller.* Dyslexia Help. http://dyslexiahelp.umich.edu/success-stories/nelson-rockefeller

University of Michigan. (n.d.). *Nolan Ryan.* Dyslexia Help. http://dyslexiahelp.umich.edu/success-stories/nolan-ryan

University of Michigan. (n.d.). *Steve Redgrave.* Dyslexia Help. http://dyslexiahelp.umich.edu/steve-redgrave

University of Michigan. (n.d.). *Tim Tebow.* Dyslexia Help. http://dyslexiahelp.umich.edu/success-stories/tim-tebow

Waber, B. (2018). *Courage.* Houghton Mifflin Harcourt.

Wade, C. (2021). *What the road said* (L. de Moyencourt, Illus.). St. Martin's Press.

White, C. I. (2018). *Grandpa and the library: How Charles White learned to paint.* The Museum of Modern Art.

Willems, M. (2003). *The pigeon.* Hyperion Books for Children.

Willems, M. (2009). *Elephant & Piggie.* Walker.

Witek, J. (2014). *In my heart: A book of feelings* (C. Roussey, Illus.). Harry N. Abrams.

Yamada, K. (2021). *Trying* (E. Hurst, Illus.). Compendium.

Yamada, K. (2021). *What do you do with a problem?* (M. Besom, Illus.). Library Ideas.

Yorkey, M. (n.d.). *Playing with purpose.* Barbour Publishing.

ACKNOWLEDGMENTS

Thank you to Dr. Rod Nicolson, whose work inspired the creation of this program.

Thank you to Michelle Kishimoto, whose introduction connected me to Liz Trudeau.

Thank you to Liz Trudeau, for believing in this program from the beginning and for partnering together in this journey to raise the self-esteem of students with dyslexia.

Thank you to Pat Pomaro, whose encouragement prompted this program into existence.

Thank you to Claudia Beeny, whose belief in me to shine inspires me to daily use my S.H.I.N.E.

Thank you to Nancy Disterlic, Kay Peterson, Courtney Nelson, Laura Jeffryes, Leigh Kapos, Beth Hewett, Debbie Wagner, and Whitney Johannessen, for not only believing in me and this program, but for also providing valuable feedback.

Thank you to Paul Trudeau, who took the ideas in my head and illustrated them so well on paper.

Thank you to Becky Noelle, whose editing skills enhanced each lesson and who I would love to sit with and have a cup of tea.

Thank you to Kristine Brogno, whose creative design work added beauty and warmth and who patiently helped me through the first semester of French class.

Thank you to S. Robin Larin, for her meticulous attention to proofreading details.

Thank you to William, Ethan, and Zach for their valuable contributions.

Thank you to Kim Vavra, Janell Peterson, and Carrie Perkins, whose prayers, support, and laughter carried me through each draft.

Thank you to my husband Ted, whose constant love and grace encourage me each day, and to my children Teddy and Sophie, whose love and laughter fill my heart with gratefulness to be their mom.

And lastly, thank you to my former and current students, whose strengths inspire me to do what I do.

For additional information:
www.brilliantstrengths.com

Join the Brilliant Strengths Community
Facebook: www.facebook.com/brilliantstrengths
Instagram: @brilliantstrengths

For inquiries
regarding the book
or speaking engagements:
info@brilliantstrengths.com

To obtain your copy
of *Brilliantly Dyslexic*, visit
brilliantlydyslexic.com
or amazon.com

www.ingramcontent.com/pod-product-compliance
Lightning Source LLC
Chambersburg PA
CBHW042346030426
42335CB00031B/3478